Little Tommy Tucker

A Pantomime

Paul Reakes

A Samuel French Acting Edition

SAMUELFRENCH-LONDON.CO.UK
SAMUELFRENCH.COM

Copyright © 2004 by Paul Reakes
All Rights Reserved

LITTLE TOMMY TUCKER is fully protected under the copyright laws of the British Commonwealth, including Canada, the United States of America, and all other countries of the Copyright Union. All rights, including professional and amateur stage productions, recitation, lecturing, public reading, motion picture, radio broadcasting, television and the rights of translation into foreign languages are strictly reserved.

ISBN 978-0-573-16445-3

www.samuelfrench-london.co.uk

www.samuelfrench.com

FOR AMATEUR PRODUCTION ENQUIRIES

UNITED KINGDOM AND WORLD
EXCLUDING NORTH AMERICA
plays@SamuelFrench-London.co.uk
020 7255 4302/01

Each title is subject to availability from Samuel French,
depending upon country of performance.

CAUTION: Professional and amateur producers are hereby warned that LITTLE TOMMY TUCKER is subject to a licensing fee. Publication of this play does not imply availability for performance. Both amateurs and professionals considering a production are strongly advised to apply to the appropriate agent before starting rehearsals, advertising, or booking a theatre. A licensing fee must be paid whether the title is presented for charity or gain and whether or not admission is charged.

The professional rights in this play are controlled by Samuel French Ltd, 52 Fitzroy Street, London, W1T 5JR.

No one shall make any changes in this title for the purpose of production. No part of this book may be reproduced, stored in a retrieval system, or transmitted in any form, by any means, now known or yet to be invented, including mechanical, electronic, photocopying, recording, videotaping, or otherwise, without the prior written permission of the publisher. No one shall upload this title, or part of this title, to any social media websites.

The right of Paul Reakes to be identified as author of this work has been asserted by him in accordance with Section 77 of the Copyright, Designs and Patents Act 1988

LITTLE TOMMY TUCKER

First presented by the Teignmouth Players at the Carlton Theatre, Teignmouth, Devon, with the following cast:

Dame Ditty	James Moffatt
Melody	Michelle Buckley
Doctor Discord	Peter Hollands
Benny	Tom Rayfield
The Duke of Sterling	Myrana Searle
Sophie	Sarah Mallett
Boy	Emma Wonnacott/Emily Burton
Tommy Tucker	Tracy Burton
Mother Curseum	Gay White
Primrose	Peter Chadwick
Professor Wizo	Harold Hayden
Judge	David Potter

Directed by **Sonia Hollands**
Musical Director **Eric Searle**

CHARACTERS

Dame Ditty, a teacher of singing
Melody, Dame's star pupil
Doctor Discord, a rival teacher
Benny
The Duke of Sterling
Sophie, Duke's daughter
A Boy
Tommy Tucker
Mother Curseum, a witch
Primrose, Curseum's assistant
Professor Wizo, a magician
A Judge

Chorus of **Townsfolk**, **Children**, **Girl Pupils**, **Goblins**, **Imps**, **Demons**, **Fairground Folk** and **Fairground Dancers**

SYNOPSIS OF SCENES

ACT I

SCENE 1   The town square
SCENE 2   A street
SCENE 3   The woods

ACT II

SCENE 1   Dame Ditty's garden
SCENE 2   The street
SCENE 3   The fairground
SCENE 4   The singing lesson
SCENE 5   The Finale

MUSICAL NUMBERS

ACT I

No. 1	**Song and Dance**	Melody, Chorus and Dancers
No. 2	**Song**	Dame, Melody, Pupils and Chorus
No. 3	**Song**	Melody and Benny
No. 4	**Song**	Dame, Melody and Audience
No. 5	**Romantic Duet**	Tommy and Sophie
No. 5a	**Reprise of Song 5**	Tommy
No. 5b	**Reprise of Song 5**	Tommy
No. 6	**Song and Dance**	Principals, Chorus and Dancers
No. 7	**Comedy Duet**	Melody and Benny
No. 8	**Song and Dance**	Principals, Chorus and Dancers
No. 9	**Comedy Duet**	Dame and Duke
No. 10	**Dance**	Imps and Demon Dancers
No. 11	**Song and Dance**	Chorus and Dancers

ACT II

No. 12	**Song and Dance**	Melody, Pupils, Chorus and Dancers
No. 13	**Song**	Dame, Melody, Tommy and Audience
No. 14	**Song**	Sophie and Chorus
No. 15	**Song and Dance**	Chorus and Dancers
No. 15a	**Reprise of Song 3**	Benny
No. 16	**Song**	Tommy
No. 17	**Song and Dance**	Principals, Chorus and Dancers
No. 18	**House Song**	Dame, Melody, Benny and Audience
No. 19	**Finale Song (Reprise)**	All

CHARACTERS AND COSTUMES

Dame Ditty (Dame) is a teacher of music and singing. This is amazing, because to look at her you wouldn't think she could tell a music sheet from a bed sheet! She is prone to "mood swings", but is basically a lovable old girl. She is always on friendly and confidential terms with the audience and never misses an opportunity of involving them. All her costumes, hairdos and make-up should be funny and outrageous. Special Finale Costume.

Melody is the Dame's star pupil. You have the feeling that she was already an accomplished singer before Dame Ditty laid claim to teaching her all she knows. She is a pretty, considerate and very sensible young woman. An excellent singing voice and dancing ability is needed for the part. Her costumes are neat and attractive, but never fussy. Finale Costume.

Doctor Discord is a rival music teacher. Although he boasts qualifications and credentials, his school is empty of pupils. This comes as no surprise when we discover that he is a slimy, sneering, scowling, obnoxious individual! He takes great pleasure in bullying Benny, consorting with witches and aggravating the audience. He wears a tight-fitting suit of unrelieved black, and his long, wild hair is brushed back from his forehead. He rather resembles Beethoven—on one of his really bad days!

Benny is Discord's downtrodden odd-job man. He is a gormless, but very lovable young yokel. The rough treatment he receives at the hands of Discord gets him the full sympathy of the audience, especially from the youngsters. Normally his singing voice is atrocious, but under the influence of the witch, he sings remarkably well. His costumes should be comically ill-fitting and tatty. Finale Costume.

The Duke of Sterling is a plump and pleasant personage. Although one of the aristocracy, he enjoys the company of the common folk. That is, until he has to cope with the amorous advances of Dame Ditty! Then he wishes he'd never left his stately home! He is well-dressed, as befitting a gentleman of his age and position.

Sophie is his daughter. A beautiful young lady. She is full of charm and grace, and is certainly not a "snob". She sings and dances extremely well, and all her costumes are exquisite. She is altogether a joy to behold. But! This is not all that is required to play the part! When Curseum, the witch, changes herself into Sophie, (for the purpose of tricking Tommy into drinking the magic potion) the actress playing Sophie is required to "double". Although unchanged in appearance, she must be able to assume the characteristics, mannerisms and voice of Curseum. A challenging role for a confident and versatile player. Finale Costume.

The Boy is a cheeky little urchin with a nonchalant air and a permanent sniff. Scruffy, untidy costumes.

Tommy Tucker (Principal Boy) is a handsome, debonair young fellow. He has a winning smile, an engaging personality and a great pair of legs! Apart from these attributes, he also possesses a magnificent singing voice. (Except when he is under the witch's spell!) A strong, charismatic player is needed for the role. His costume is pantomime "shabby". Splendid Finale Costume.

Mother Curseum, the witch. This is a "lady" you wouldn't want to upset—even if she didn't have magical powers! She is a thoroughly nasty piece of work who revels in her own malevolence and sarcastic sense of humour. A strong character comedienne is needed, one who can stand up to the audience and give as good as she gets. Her costume and make-up can be traditional with pointed hat, hooked nose and warts, etc., or let your costume designer dream up something really weird and outlandish.

Primrose is Curseum's assistant. She (the part can be played by a male) is a very odd and bizarre looking individual. Hardly human, comically grotesque and sporting a mass of unruly hair—and not all of it on her head! She is only required to wheel on the cauldron, grunt, nod, and do a few lumbering dance steps.

Professor Wizo, the magician. Although extremely ancient and doddery, he certainly knows his magical onions (when he remembers to bring the right book of spells, that is). He is full of old world charm, cultivated of speech and still has an eye for the girls. He has a long white beard and peers out through thick spectacles. As he had to leave his house in a hurry, he wears a tasselled smoking cap, velvet smoking jacket, check trousers and carpet slippers. For the Finale he wears his full magician's regalia with pointed hat and gown decorated with magical signs and symbols.

A Judge, for the singing contest. This can be played by a member of the Chorus, either male or female. However, it would be a nice touch if you could persuade a well-known local personality to dress up and undertake the role. It is non-speaking and only appears towards the end of Act II.

The Chorus, Children and **Dancers** have plenty to do appearing as townsfolk, children, girl pupils, demons, imps, ghouls, zombies, fairground folk and fairground dancers.

Other works by Paul Reakes
published by Samuel French Ltd

Pantomimes:

Babes in the Wood
Bluebeard
Dick Turpin
King Arthur
Little Jack Horner
Little Miss Muffet
Little Red Riding Hood
Old Mother Hubbard
Robinson Crusoe and the Pirates
Santa in Space
Sinbad the Sailor

Plays:

Bang, You're Dead!
Mantrap

PRODUCTION NOTES

STAGING

The pantomime offers opportunities for elaborate staging, but can be produced quite simply if facilities and funds are limited.

There are four full sets:
 The Town Square
 The Woods
 Dame Ditty's Garden
 The Fairground

All these scenes are interlinked with tabs or frontcloth scenes (one only—The Street).

The last set can be used for the Finale with the removal of the platform and chairs.

LIGHTING AND EFFECTS

The lighting for the first two scenes of Act I is straightforward and plain sailing. However, in Act I, Scene 3 (The Woods) there are plenty of opportunities for some really spectacular "out of this world" lighting and sound effects. Thunder and lightning, weird flashing lights, uncanny noises, eerie spotlights, ghostly ground mist, etc.—the works! This is used for the entrance of the witch and her demons, the brewing of the magic potion and the casting of the evil spell, etc. Let your lighting and effects crew pull out all the stops for this particular scene. For Act II, the lighting and sound is fairly straightforward, apart from the occasional flash, puff of smoke and blackout. Extra use of follow spots for musical numbers, etc., is left to the individual director. Taped sound of "eerie" organ music and a fairground organ is also required.

ACT I

Scene 1

The Town Square

Prominent R is Dame Ditty's house with a practical front door and a hanging sign, which reads "DAME DITTY. SINGING LESSONS GIVEN". Prominent L is Dr Discord's house with a practical front door and a far more elaborate sign, which reads "DOCTOR DISCORD. R.A.M. SUPERIOR TEACHER OF MUSIC AND SINGING". Other houses and shops as side wings. The back cloth shows the rest of the town. Across the back hangs a banner, reading "FAIR! TODAY!"

When the CURTAIN *rises, Melody and the Chorus, as Townsfolk and Children, are discovered. They go straight into the opening song and dance*

Song 1

After the number, Dame Ditty bustles from her house

Dame (*to the Chorus, very bright and breezy*) Good morning, good morning, good morning!
All Morning, Dame Ditty!
Dame (*spotting the audience*) Oh, I say! Look! We've got company! (*To the audience, preening herself*) Oh, whatever must you think! Me without a speck of make-up on, an' me 'air lookin' like a bird's nest! Melody, why didn't you tell me we 'ad visitors?
Melody I've only just noticed them myself, Dame Ditty. (*To the audience, politely*) Hallo.

A few replies from the audience

Dame Oh, dear, oh, dear! (*To Melody*) Not very sociable, are they? P'raps they're from [local place]. They don't understand proper English there. I'll 'ave a go! (*Shouting at the audience*) Hallo!!

The audience shout back

(*To the audience*) I still can't hear! (*Shouting at them*) Hallo!!

The audience shout back, even louder

That's more like it! My word, you've got a good set of lungs on ya! And I should know because I've got a marvellous pair meself. Look! (*Comic business as she thrusts her bosom out and parades up and down*) Wonderful, aren't they? Can you see them at the back? (*Comic business and ad lib*) Oh, yes, you need a good pair of lungs in my job! I teach singing, y'see. (*She points up to her sign*) Dame Ditty—that's me! (*She does a few "tra la la"s which ends in a fit of coughing*) I really must stop smokin' that pipe! I'm the best singing teacher in town. Oh, there is another one—but 'e's rubbish! (*She goes and points up to Discord's sign, with disgust*) Dr Discord! That's him! (*To the Chorus*) He's not a nice man, is he?

All (*grimacing*) No!

Dame (*to the audience*) No, 'e's 'orrible an' slimy! He makes [current nasty] look like [current heart throb]! (*She reads the sign*) R.A.M.! D'you know what that stands for? Rotten and mouldy!

Dame Ditty and the others laugh

Oh, 'e might give himself fancy letters after 'is name, but for the best results, I'm yer man! Take young Melody 'ere. I taught her all she knows, and she's a wonderful singist! My star pupil! I've got other ones as well. Where are they? Girls?

A bunch of Girls come forward

(*Proudly*) Ah! Here they are! My pupils! Aren't they lovely? (*To a Girl who is scratching her nose*) Don't do that, dear! (*To the audience*) All budding [current singer]! Say hallo to our visitors, girls.

Girls (*to the audience, in half-hearted mumbles*) Hallo.

Dame (*appalled*) Quiver me quavers! (*She mimics them*) Hallo! That's not how I taught you to articulate! Breathe properly first! (*To a Girl*) And stop chewing, Ermintrude!

The Girl swallows hard

Now! All of you take a deep breath! Breathe—*in*!

The Girls do so. Dame turns away and chats to the audience

They're a bit young to appreciate the finer points of singing. They still think

Act I, Scene 1

a tenor is somethin' you get from a cash point! Their 'eads are too full of S Club 7 [or the name of a current group, mispronounced]. That's the trouble! But they're not a bad bunch, really. Why, only the other day one of them actually——

By this time the Girls are at bursting point. One of them pulls at Dame Ditty's dress to attract her attention

What? (*She turns with alarm*) Oh! Out! Out!

The Girls breathe out and start gasping and coughing

(*Appalled again*) Crumple me crochets! You sound like the [local pub] at chuckin' out time! Really, girls! I've been tellin' our visitors how good we are! What'll they think!
Melody Instead of *telling* them how good we are, why don't we *show* them.
Dame What, give 'em a demonstration, y'mean?

Melody nods

What a good idea! (*To the audience*) You'd like that, wouldn't you?

The audience responds

Yes, I knew you would (*or*) too bad, 'cos you're gonna get it! (*To the Chorus*) You lot can join in as well. You've all been pupils of mine in the past. (*She pulls a Male forward*) I remember *you*! A right Basso Profondo, you were! (*She pushes the man back and turns to Melody*) What song shall we sing for them?
Melody Why not the one we've been rehearsing.
Dame Right! (*To the others, clapping her hands*) Places everyone! Places!

Melody and the Girls form a group c. The Chorus fill the back. Dame comes forward to address the pianist or conductor

Now, do you think you can manage this? You can. Good! (*To the audience, confidentially*) Only [s]he's had a bit of trouble, y'see. Infestation in his/ her upright! (*Ultra posh*) Hand now—for your hedification and delight— we proudly present our rendering of [chosen song]! (*She goes up to the group and turns her back to the audience, preparing to conduct. She looks over her shoulder. To the audience*) Excuse my back! (*She turns to the Group*) Excuse my front! Everybody ready! (*She raises her arms*) And——

Song 2

Despite Dame Ditty's comic antics as a conductor, a very pleasant sound comes from Melody, the Girls and the Chorus. It is only marred when Dame Ditty decides to sing a solo! However, the others soon drown her out and the number ends well. All bow to the audience. Dame Ditty curtsies and waves like a prima donna

Dr Discord comes from his house

Discord What was that hideous cacophony? It sounded like someone twisting a cat's tail! (*He sees the Dame and the Group*) Oh, I might have known! (*With sneering contempt*) It's Julie Andrews and the Von Trapp family!
Dame (*to the audience*) That's him! Yuck! (*She goes to Discord with mock reverence*) Why, if it isn't Dr Discord, R.A.M.

Slight pause

Rotten and mouldy!

Dame and the others roar with laughter

Discord Bah! How dare you ridicule my credentials!
Dame I wouldn't touch 'em with a barge pole, or any other part of you! Ugh!!
Discord (*sneering*) Well, at least I *have* credentials. *I* am qualified to teach music and singing. You're not! You're just an ex member of [local musical comedy society]! And back row of the chorus at that! (*He gives an unpleasant chuckle*)
Dame (*indignantly*) I'll 'ave you know, my *Chu Chin Chow* is still talked about!
Discord Yes, so is the *Titanic*! Pah! You're not fit to teach *gargling* let alone singing! (*Another unpleasant chuckle*)
Dame Oh! If I wasn't a lady I'd slosh you one for that!
Discord Ha! If you're a lady, I'm Carol Vorderman! You're a big fraud, that's what you are!
Dame Ooh! A fraud, am I?! Well, you just ask our visitors! They know what a good teacher I am! (*To the audience*) Don't you, folks?

"Yes!" from the audience

Discord (*to the audience; sneering*) Bah! *Your* opinion doesn't matter! You all look tone deaf to me—the *live* ones, that is! (*Again the unpleasant cackle*)

Act I, Scene 1

Dame (*to the audience*) See! I told you 'e was a rotten so-an-so!
Discord (*to her; with venom*) You're a charlatan! You're unqualified, unprofessional and ... and unattractive!
Dame (*enraged*) Ooh! Why, you... (*To Melody*) 'Old me back! 'Old me back!
Melody If that's true, Doctor, how can you explain the fact that Dame Ditty has a class full of pupils, and you don't have a single one.

This deflates Discord. The Chorus voice their agreement

Dame Nice one, Melody! (*To Discord, very cockily*) Yes, Mr Know-all-knickers! How do you explain that?

Discord is obviously stumped. Dame and the others jeer and taunt him. In desperation, he snarls at them

Discord It's not true!! (*With false bravado*) Why, only this morning I have taken on a most promising pupil. He shows enormous potential.
Dame Never mind 'ow big 'e is! Where is he? Let's see him!
Chorus Yes! Bring him out! Where is he? (*Etc.*)
Discord (*floundering*) Well, I ... I...
Melody (*tongue-in-cheek*) What's the matter, Doctor? Is he shy?
Dame He's so shy, 'e's invisible! (*To Discord*) Be honest! There isn't any pupil, is there?
Discord (*snarling*) Oh, yes, there is!
Dame
Others } (*together*) Oh, no, there isn't!

"Oh, yes, there is!"/"Oh, no, there isn't!" routine follows, involving the audience

Dame (*to Discord, after the routine has run its course*) All right, then! Prove it! Bring 'im out!
Discord Very well! I will! (*He goes to the door of his house and calls inside*) Hey, you! Yes, *you*! Come out here at once!

Benny, a likeable, but gormless young man, appears in the doorway. He wears a small, frilly apron, and carries a bucket and cloth. When he sees that all eyes are on him, he makes to dive back into the house. Discord pulls him back out

Benny (*with a nervous grin*) 'Ullo.
Discord (*bringing Benny forward*) Here he is! My promising new pupil!
Benny Eh?!

Discord (*aside to Benny*) Be quiet! (*To Dame, boastfully*) You see! I told you I had one!
Dame (*going to Benny and looking at him*) Ye-es. 'E looks like a right one!
Benny 'Ullo. (*He grins at her inanely*)
Dame (*to the audience*) Move over, Einstein! (*To Benny*) What's your name?
Benny (*stumped*) Er ... er...
Dame (*to the audience*) Talk about the *weakest* link! This one's the *missing* link!
Benny It's Benny!
Discord Short for Benedetto. He has Italian blood.
Benny Eh?!

Discord gives him a quick jab in the ribs

Dame Really? Where does 'e keep it? In that bucket?
Discord Many great singers come from Italy.
Benny (*to Dame, brightly*) I come from [local place]!

Discord jabs him again

Dame (*to the audience*) That accounts for it!
Discord This young man could be a second Pavarotti.
Dame Did you say *rotti* or *grotty*? (*To Benny*) Go on, then. Let's hear you sing.

The Chorus voice their agreement

Benny (*panicking*) Sing! But I come to clean the...
Discord (*jabbing him*) Be quiet! (*To Dame*) I ... er ... don't want him to strain his voice.
Dame Why not? 'E looks like 'e's strained everything else! (*Mockingly*) Yah! *He's* no singer! You're 'avin' us on! You're all wind and pizzicato!

Dame and the others jeer at Discord. He drags Benny aside and speaks in hushed tones

Discord Listen, dunderhead! You've got to sing to them!
Benny But I can't sing! I only come 'ere to clean your windows!
Discord (*viciously*) If you don't do as I say, I will throw you and your mother out of that cottage!
Benny (*horrified*) You wouldn't!
Discord Oh, yes, I would!

Benny (*resigned*) A'right then.
Discord (*aloud, to the others*) Very well, you disbelieving dolts! Benedetto has agreed to show you his prowess.
Dame (*to the audience*) Better send the kids home!
Discord (*taking the bucket and cloth from Benny, announcing grandly*) Sing to them, Benedetto—(*aside to Benny*) or else! (*He pushes Benny forward*)

Nervously, Benny looks around, and grins at the expectant crowd. He clears his throat several times, then bursts into song. (The refrain of a popular song, unaccompanied.) It is an appalling, off-key noise! Dame Ditty and the others groan and put their fingers in their ears. Discord is enraged, but tries to keep face. Eventually, Benny drifts into embarrassed silence. The others laugh and jeer at him

Dame (*to the others*) I don't think [current singer]'s got anything to worry about, do you? (*To Discord*) I knew he'd be rubbish!

More laughter and jeers. Taking pity on him, Melody crosses to Benny

Melody I expect you're just feeling a little nervous.

Benny turns, and sees her for the first time. He is obviously greatly smitten and gawps at her, open-mouthed

I'm one of Dame Ditty's pupils. My name is Melody.
Benny (*flustered*) Er... Perry meased to pleat you...

Melody holds out her hand to him. Benny just gawps at it, then wipes his own hand on his apron and bashfully takes hers. His reaction is one of utter bliss

Melody Perhaps you'd like me to give you a hand.
Benny (*dumbly, looking at her hand which he still holds*) I fought you already 'ad! But I don't mind takin' the other one as well. (*With a soppy grin, he takes her other hand. Double bliss!*)
Melody (*smiling*) I meant—give you a hand with your singing.
Benny Oh! (*He drops her hands and gives a dopey laugh. Then he turns to her, seriously*) Oh, yes, please—Melody. You show me 'ow to do it.

Song 3

A song, in which Benny only has to sing simple responses. No great demands on his vocal talent! Dame Ditty and the Others can join in if so desired. After, they all applaud Melody and Benny. He is very pleased with himself

Discord (*making the most of the applause*) There! You see! I told you he had a fine voice!
Dame Come off it! Without Melody's help he'd have been total rubbish! If he's your only pupil, you'd better shut up shop right now!

The Chorus agree, then laugh and jeer at Discord. Angrily, he drags Benny to DL, *and thrusts the bucket and cloth at him. Dame Ditty and Melody clear to* DR

The Duke of Sterling enters upstage. On his arm is his beautiful daughter Sophie. In awe, the Chorus move aside to allow the finely-dressed couple to advance forward

Duke (*acknowledging the Chorus as they come down*) Good morning—how de do—greetings—good morning...
Dame (*aside to Melody*) Crikey! Who are they?
Duke (*to Dame*) Ah! The top of the morning to you, dear lady. (*He gives her an elegant bow*)
Dame (*flattered and flustered*) Oh! And the top of the milk to *you*! (*She does an awkward curtsy*)
Duke I don't believe I've had the pleasure.
Dame (*fluttering her eyelashes at him*) There's plenty of time yet.
Duke (*slightly taken aback, but not offended*) Er ... yes! I am the Duke of Sterling. This is my daughter Sophie.
Sophie How do you do.
Dame (*gushing*) Oh, charmed ever so muchly! I'm Ditty.
Duke By Jove! I'm sorry to hear that.
Dame (*with a playful nudge*) No, silly! That's my name! *Dame* Ditty—(*with a nudge and a wink*) spinster.
Duke Er ... yes. We have just taken up residence of Moneybag Manor. D'you know the place at all?
Dame Oh, hintimately!
Duke Really? Have you stayed there?
Dame Only until the tour guide chucked me out! (*She nudges him and gives a "horsey" laugh*) Haw! Haw! Haw!
Sophie (*indicating Dame's sign*) I see that you give singing lessons, Dame Ditty.
Dame Oh, yus! The best in town. This is my star pupil—Melody.

Melody curtsies

Pray give the Duke an' Dukelet an earful.

Melody sings the scales beautifully. Much impressed, the Duke and Sophie applaud her. Benny joins in, until Discord stops him

Sophie (*to Melody*) Thank you. That was delightful.
Dame Trained by yours truly, of course. (*Grandly*) Dame Ditty! The best teacher in town!
Discord Pah! Codswallop!

This attracts the Duke's attention and he crosses to Discord. He looks up at his sign

Duke Egad! *Another* teacher of singing!
Discord (*with a grovelling bow*) Your Grace! This is *my* establishment. A reputable place of learning—unlike *that* one! (*He points to Dame's house*) Allow me to introduce myself. I am Dr Discord, R.A.M.
Duke What does that stand for?
Dame (*chipping in*) Rotten and mouldy!
Discord (*coughing loudly to drown her out*) Ahhemm!! They stand for—Royal Academy of Music, your Grace. With these glowing credentials it is obvious that I am the superior teacher. (*Very smarmy and grovelling*) As a man of refinement and education, I am sure your Grace will agree.
Duke Mm. Where is *your* star pupil?
Benny (*holding up his hand*) I'm 'ere!

Discord jabs him in the ribs

Duke And what is he going to give us?
Dame (*yelling across*) The earache!
Discord (*hedging*) Well... I'd rather he didn't...
Duke Come, come, Doctor! We heard Dame Ditty's pupil. And very nice it was too. Now we want to hear yours! (*To Benny*) Come, my good fellow, step forward and let us hear you!
Dame (*rubbing her hands with glee*) Ha! Ha! This is gonna be good!

Benny comes forward. Discord cringes away, unable to watch. Benny hands the bucket to the puzzled Duke

(*To the Duke*) You'll need that in a minute! (*She makes "sick making" gestures, and sniggers*)

Benny, displaying more confidence now, clears his throat and sings the scales. Again, it is an atrocious noise! The Chorus groan and stick their fingers in their ears. The Duke and Sophie wince. Discord wishes he could disappear, and Dame Ditty revels in his discomfort. Benny finishes, and beams at everyone, almost expecting a round of applause

Duke (*to Benny, stuck for words*) Er ...yes ... er ... well... (*He gives Benny the bucket*)
Discord (*trying to repair the damage*) He's not at his best today, your Grace. He has a slight frog in his throat.
Duke It sounded more like a huge toad in the hole to me!

The others roar with laughter, particularly Dame Ditty

Dame (*moving to Duke's R*) Y'see, Dukey! I told you my school's the best!
Discord (*moving to Duke's L*) But *I* have the credentials! *Mine* is the best!
Dame Mine is!
Discord Mine is!

Dame and Discord argue across the Duke. Finally, he holds up his hand to silence them

Duke Quiet—please!

Dame and Discord stop arguing and glare at each other

Egad, y'do seem to have a problem. Which school *is* the best? I only wish there was something I could do to settle the dispute for you, but...
Sophie May I make a suggestion, Papa? Why not hold a singing contest between the two schools.
Duke To decide which of 'em is the best, y'mean?
Sophie Yes. One singer could represent each school. You could find an impartial judge, and that way it would be done fairly.
Duke (*enthused*) A capital idea, m'dear! Capital! That is—if the two parties are agreeable.
Dame (*cocksure*) It suits me!
Discord (*not so!*) And me.
Duke Splendid, splendid! And I'll tell you what! We'll hold the contest this very afternoon at the fair! How would that suit you?
Dame I can't wait!
Discord (*mumbling*) Nor me.
Duke And to add a little spice to the proceedings, I will award one thousand pounds to the winning school!

General reaction. Discord turns away, and is obviously scheming

Act I, Scene 1

Dame (*to Melody; with glee*) Ha! Ha! With you singin' that thousand nicker's as good as mine already! Old face-ache won't stand a chance with 'is strangled chicken over there! (*She sidles up to the Duke, batting her eyelashes*) Thank you, Dukey. I'm sure there's some way I can show you my appreciation.

Duke (*flustered*) Oh, dear lady, I...

Sophie (*amused, but firmly*) Papa, I don't think you should be showing any favouritism, do you?

Duke What? Oh, no! (*He edges away from Dame*) Certainly not!

Discord Your Grace, I have a query.

Dame There's no answer to that!

Discord (*to Duke*) Does the contestant have to be a male or a female singer?

Duke By Jove! Does it matter?

Discord Oh, I think it does. May I suggest that it be decided on the toss of a coin? Say—heads for a male—tails for a female. (*He quickly produces a coin*) Here is a coin you can use.

Duke Oh, very well. (*He takes the coin*) Heads—male! Tails—female! (*He tosses the coin and catches it on the back of his hand. He shows them the coin*) Heads! A *male* singer it is!

Discord smirks and gives an unpleasant chuckle. Dame Ditty, realizing what this means, is far from happy

Well, that's settled! Now I must go and arrange a suitable judge for the contest. (*Offering his arm*) Come, Sophie. (*To All*) Farewell! (*To Dame*) Farewell, dear lady.

Dame Ditty is too preoccupied with her own thoughts to notice. The Duke reacts at this, then turns to exit

Discord (*stopping him*) Your Grace—my coin.

The Duke gives him the coin, and he and Sophie exit at the back

With excited chatter, the Chorus follow them out

(*With a sneering laugh*) Ha! Ha! Ha! Not so confident now, are you, Ditty? You haven't got a male in your school, have you? (*He pulls Benny forward*) *I* have! Oh, he may be a tuneless cretin, but he's still a *male*!

Dame Huh! I'd like a doctor's report on that!

Discord (*sneering*) Say what you like. With him, *I'm* going to win that contest and the thousand pounds! Ha! Ha! Ha! That'll prove I'm the best teacher! (*To the audience*) Oh, yes, it will!

"Oh, no, it won't!"/"Oh, yes, it will!" routine with the audience

(*Pushing Benny towards his house*) Come on, you!
Benny I fink I'll be goin' 'ome now.
Discord You're not going anywhere until you've won me that contest! Inside!
Benny (*waving bashfully*) Goodbye, Melody.
Melody (*waving back*) Goodbye, Benny.

Discord pushes him inside, then turns to give another smirking laugh

Dame Oh, go and boil yer 'ead! You wouldn't be laughin' if that coin 'ad come up tails!
Discord No chance of that! You see—(*he holds up the coin*) it's a *two-headed* coin! Ha! Ha! Ha!

Amid boos and hisses, Discord exits into his house and slams the door

Dame (*angrily crossing to his door and calling after him*) Ooh! You ... you Jeffrey Archer, you! (*She turns back to Melody, in despair*) What are we gonna do? He's right! He's gonna win the contest with that useless Benny!
Melody I think he's rather nice.
Dame (*incredulously*) You don't mean to say you fancy that gormless article! (*To the audience*) Tch! I dunno! Girls these days! (*To Melody*) Well, never mind that! What are we gonna do? We can't let old misery guts win!
Melody There's only one thing we *can* do. We've got to find a male singer before this afternoon.
Dame Huh! That'll be like tryin' to find a straight corkscrew [or local topical gag]!

A small Boy, with his hands in his pockets, saunters on from DR

Melody (*pointing the boy out to Dame*) What about him?
Dame (*looking*) But 'e's only a little shrimp!
Melody They didn't specify how old the male had to be.
Dame That's true! (*She calls to the Boy, very sweetly*) Yoo hoo! Little boy! Come here a moment.

The Boy saunters across to her, still with his hands in his pockets

Boy Watch'er! (*He gives a loud sniff*)
Dame Now, my little man. Can you sing?

Act I, Scene 1   13

Boy Yeah! (*Sniff*) Like a bird! (*Sniff*)
Dame (*aside to Melody*) One with foul pest by the sound of it! (*To Boy*) How would you like to sing for me in the contest?
Boy Don't mind. (*Sniff*)
Dame Good! (*Sniff. To the audience*) Crikey! It's catchin'!
Boy 'Ow much? (*Sniff*)
Dame 'Ow much what? (*Sniff*)
Boy 'Ow much do I get paid fer singin'? (*Sniff*)
Dame Er... I'll give you fifty pence.
Boy Fifty pence! (*Sniff*) You mus' be jokin'!
Dame All right then! I'll make it a pound!
Boy (*sniffing*) Is that yer final offer?
Dame It is! (*Sniff*) It's not to be sniffed at. (*To the audience*) What am I sayin'!
Boy So long then! (*Sniff*)

Boy saunters away towards DR *exit*

Dame (*calling after him*) Oy! Does that mean you're not interested?
Boy Got it in one!

With a final sniff, Boy saunters off DR

Dame (*to the audience*) How d'you like that! Cheeky little—I 'ope 'e's not with you!
Melody You should have offered him more money.
Dame I know what I *should* 'ave offered 'im! (*In despair again*) Oh, it's hopeless! We're not gonna find anyone in time!
Melody (*indicating the audience*) What about our visitors? Perhaps one of them would be nice enough to help us out.

Bring up House Lights

Dame Oh, that's a great idea! (*To the audience*) Now then! Who'd like to 'elp me win that contest and beat old Mr Nasty? Sorry, but it's got to be someone of the male agenda. Don't worry, girls, you'll get your chance later on. What I need is a little boy, or even—a *big* boy! Yes, that includes the dads! (*Ad lib and by play with the audience*) Now, I'd like you all to come up 'ere for an audition. That means I want to see what you're made of! Come on, don't be shy!
Melody I think we'd better go and fetch them.

Ad lib and comic business as Dame and Melody go down and collect men and boys from the auditorium, and take them on to the stage. Dame can make comments to the wives, like: "I'll let you 'ave 'im back later, dear—when I've finished with 'im!" etc., etc.! They arrange the group and ask their names and ages, etc.

Dame (*to a man*) Don't look so worried, dear! I 'aven't got me castin' couch with me! (*To another man, indicating Melody*) Neither has *she*, so take that twinkle out of yer eye, you naughty boy! Now, let's start this audition!

The choice of how to play this is left to the individual director. The following are only suggestions: (A) The individual men and boys could sing something of their own choosing, (B) Melody could bring on the song sheet of a simple song for them to sing to, (C) Dame Ditty and Melody could sing something and get each one to sing the responses

Song 4

Dame (*to the group*) I've now got to decide which of you song birds is goin' to sing for me in the contest. Excuse me while I go and cogitate! (*To a man*) That's "'ave a think" to you!

Dame takes Melody to one side, and they converse in whispers

(*Going back to the group*) Well! You will be delighted to learn that I have chosen—(*pregnant pause*) none of you! Ahh! (*She sighs and gets the audience to join in*)

Melody exits

You all did very well, but you don't quite 'ave what I'm after. (*To a man*) Even *you*! (*To all*) But you're not going away empty-handed...

Melody returns with sweets, etc.

She and Dame Ditty hand them to the men and boys. Some can be thrown out into the audience

(*To the audience*) Let's give them a nice big clap!

The audience applaud. Dame and Melody take the men and boys back to their seats, then return to the stage

Take out House Lights

That was a complete waste of time!
Melody Never mind. We mustn't give up. We've *got* to find someone. Let's try down [local] Street.
Dame (*sarcastically*) Oh, yes! Perhaps Robbie Williams or Elton John are 'angin' about with nothin' to do!

With a shrug to the audience, Dame follows Melody out DL

The fine, melodious voice of Tommy Tucker is heard off stage (unaccompanied). He strolls on from UR. *He is a handsome, cheerful young fellow, wearing picturesque, but shabby clothing. Still singing, and looking about him, he strolls* DC. *He sees the audience and greets them cordially*

Tommy Oh, hallo there! I'm sorry, I didn't realize there was anyone here. How are you all? Good! I've only just arrived in town. I've been spending a couple of days in a place called [local place]. Do you know it? Exactly! They told me to move on! So here I am! This seems like a nice place. Is it a nice place?

Sophie enters from DL. *She is looking in her bag, and doesn't notice Tommy*

He notices her—and how

(*To the audience*) Cor! I should say it is! (*He moves to Sophie and removes his hat*) Good morning.
Sophie (*looking up, surprised*) Oh! Good morning.

A pause as they gaze into each other's eyes. It is obviously love at first sight

Tommy (*coming down to earth*) Er ... are you a yokel... I mean, a local?
Sophie Only recently. Are you?
Tommy No.
Sophie Oh!

An awkward pause

Tommy I'm sorry. Do forgive me. My name is Tucker. But, you can call me Tommy ... because it's my name.
Sophie I'm very pleased to meet you—Tommy. My name is Sophie.
Tommy Sophie! What a lovely name.
Sophie Thank you. I've had it a long time.
Tommy I hope you'll forgive my shabby appearance.

Sophie Please don't mention it. Are you on a walking holiday?
Tommy Oh, no. I'm travelling the world, looking for my true destiny.
Sophie (*laughing*) Oh, good heavens!
Tommy I really am.
Sophie (*realizing he is serious*) I'm sorry. And have you found it—your true destiny?
Tommy Oh, yes. At last I think I have. (*He takes her hands, gazes into her eyes and sings*)

Song 5

A romantic duet and dance with romantic lighting. After the number, the couple embrace

Duke (*off* DL; *calling*) Sophie? Sophie?

The couple part, as the Duke enters from DL

Ah, there you are, m'dear... (*He sees Tommy*) Oh!
Sophie Papa, allow me to introduce Mr Tommy Tucker. (*To Tommy*) This is my father—the Duke of Sterling.

Tommy bows to the Duke, who bows back. Tommy bows again, so does the Duke. Comic business as they keep bowing to each other. Finally, the Duke gets dizzy

Duke (*to Sophie*) I've made arrangements for the contest judge, m'dear. There's just time for a constitutional before luncheon. (*He offers her his arm*) Good day, Mr ... er...
Tommy Tucker. (*He bows*)

The Duke is about to resume the bowing business, but checks himself

Duke Er ... yes ... come, Sophie. (*He leads her towards the exit* DR)

Sophie pauses to look back at Tommy

Sophie Good day.
Tommy Good day.

Sophie and the Duke exit DR

(*To the audience, ecstatically*) Oh, and *what* a good day it is, folks! I'm in

Act I, Scene 1   17

love! Hopelessly, desperately, and head over heels in love! She's lovely, isn't she? A dream, a vision, a... (*Suddenly he comes down to earth*) A daughter of a Duke! And look at me! Tatty Tommy Tucker without a penny to my name! I wish I had some money to buy some decent clothes, then I could ask her out. (*Rapturously*) Oh, Sophie! (*He sings a short reprise of Song 5*)

Song 5a (Reprise)

Unseen by Tommy, Dame Ditty and Melody enter from DL

They pull up short on hearing the sound of his voice and stand listening. Tommy finishes singing and moves DR, *where he looks off, longingly*

Dame (*to Melody*) Are you thinkin' what I'm thinkin'?
Melody With a voice like that he's bound to win. Quick! Ask him before he goes away.

They both move towards Tommy

Dame (*crossing*) Hallo, young man!
Tommy (*turning*) Oh! Hallo—hallo.
Dame We couldn't 'elp observin' you just now. You 'ave a magnificent vocal organ.
Tommy I'm sorry. (*He checks his costume*) I didn't realize it was showing.
Dame I meant your singin' voice. It's superb!
Melody It's marvellous!
Dame It's stupendous!
Tommy (*flattered*) Thank you very much. I've always been a bit of a warbler. I think my mum must have fed me on birdseed as a baby.
Dame I'm Ditty.
Tommy Oh, I'm sorry to hear that.
Dame We've already used that one! Dame Ditty—teacher of singing! This is my star pupil, Melody.
Tommy Pleased to meet you both. I'm Tommy Tucker.
Dame Well, listen, Tommy Tucker. How would you like to represent my school in an all-male singing contest this afternoon?
Tommy A singing contest! I... I've never done anything like that before.
Dame Oh, you can't lose! There's only one other contestant, an' 'e's rubbish.
Tommy (*shaking his head*) Thanks for asking me, but I don't think so.
Melody (*pulling Dame aside*) Tell him about the money.
Dame What money?
Melody The prize money. The thousand pounds.

Dame Shh! I was 'opin' not to bring that up!
Melody You've got to offer him half.
Dame (*gulping*) 'Alf!
Melody He needs an incentive.
Dame And I need me 'ead read! Oh, I suppose you're right. After all, it's beatin' old Discord that really counts, isn't it? (*She goes to Tommy*) Er ... you may be interested to know that there is a cash prize. A thousand pounds. If we win, I'm prepared to give you one——

Melody nudges her

——two——

Melody nudges her again

——five hundred pounds!
Tommy Five hundred pounds! (*To the audience*) I'd be able to buy some smart gear in [local shop], and ask Sophie out! (*To Dame*) All right! Dame Ditty, you've got yourself a singer!
Dame (*yelling with joy*) Hurray! Yipeeee!! (*She shakes Tommy's hand and slaps him on the back*)

The Chorus enter from various directions, wondering what all the fuss is about

Discord comes from his house, followed by Benny without his bucket and cloth

Discord (*to Dame; sneering*) What have you got to be so happy about? I thought you'd be packing your bags and emigrating to [local place] by now!
Dame (*singing and dancing about in front of Discord*) I'm going to win! I'm going to wi-in! I'm going to wi-in!
Discord (*mimicking her*) Oh, no, you're no-ot! Oh, no you're no-ot! You'll never find a singer in time for the contest.
Dame Oh, but I have, cheeky chops! (*She slaps his cheeks, then turns to Tommy*) And here he is! (*She brings Tommy forward*) Allow me to present my contestant—Mr Tommy Tucker!

Tommy takes a bow. General reaction

Discord (*sneering*) So! You managed to find a dim-wit to help you out. But can he sing?

Act I, Scene 2

Dame Can Homer Simpson eat doughnuts! Tommy—sing!

Again, Tommy sings a short reprise of Song 5

Song 5b (Reprise)

When he has finished, Dame Ditty holds up Tommy's arm like a prize fighter's. Wild excitement and applause from the others. Discord is beside himself with disbelief and anger. He rounds on Benny, who is applauding Tommy with the others

Dame (*to Discord*) What d'you say now?
Discord (*fuming and speechless*) I... I... Bah!!

Discord stomps into his house and slams the door

All the others laugh

Dame Tommy, I've only ever heard you sing that one song. You must know some others.
Tommy Oh, plenty! How about this one!

Song 6

A lively song and dance that involves the Principals and Chorus. The number ends with a tableau, as the Lights fade to Black-out

Music to cover the Scene change, then the Lights come up on

Scene 2

A street

Tabs, or a frontcloth showing picturesque shops and houses. There is a poster advertising the fair, with a "PLUS—GRAND SINGING CONTEST" sticker across it

Discord stomps on from DL. *He snarls at the audience and is met with the usual barrage of abuse*

Discord Bah! Curse old Ditty's luck! Where did she find that Tommy Tucker! I must admit he has a splendid voice! And what do *I* have?! Benny, the buffoon! A bullfrog with laryngitis! She'll win the contest for sure—and the thousand pounds! Bah! It's not fair, is it?

"Oh, yes, it is!"/"Oh, no, it isn't!" routine with the audience

Meanwhile, Benny drifts on from DL

Unseen by Discord, Benny joins in with the audience's responses. After a while, Discord becomes aware of him, and fixes him with an icy glare. Benny dwindles into silence, and gives a big, silly grin

What do you think you're doing?
Benny (*still grinning*) I'm tryin' to brighten the place up.
Discord You couldn't brighten up a light bulb factory! You're incompetent!
Benny Not since I bin takin' the tablets.
Discord You're two steps from an idiot!
Benny I'll move, then. (*He does so*)
Discord (*to the audience*) If you think he's so funny, why don't you have him with you!
Benny I'd like that! (*To the audience*) We're mates, aren't we? (*He gives them the thumbs up*)
Discord (*sneering*) Congratulations! You deserve each other!
Benny D'you still want me to sing for you in that contest? I bin practisin'. Listen... (*He makes an atrocious attempt at the scales*) Better innit?
Discord Better than what? No, I don't want you to sing for me. I'm withdrawing from the contest. There's no point now that Ditty has Tommy Tucker singing for her!
Benny 'E's a good singer, in 'e?
Discord Unfortunately—yes!
Benny Why don't you get 'im to sing for you?
Discord You stupid... What did you say? (*Struck by the idea*) But of course! That's it! Why didn't I think of it? Yes! I'll get Tommy Tucker to sing for *me*! (*He rubs his hands with devilish glee*) Ha! Ha! Ha! (*To Benny*) So! You do have something between your ears after all!
Benny 'Course I do—me face!
Discord You actually had an idea. All by yourself. And a good one too! Well done.
Benny (*pleased*) Ta! (*Hopefully*) Does that mean you won't ever throw me an' Mum out of the cottage?
Discord (*viciously*) I never said that! I may want something to cheer me up during the Winter months! (*He looks off* R) Ah! Here comes Tommy Tucker now, with old Ditty and that Melody.
Benny Melody! (*He sighs and goes all soppy*)

Discord We'll hide over there, and hope to catch him on his own. Come on! (*He crosses to the exit* DL)

Benny is in a daydream, thinking of Melody

Discord comes back and drags him out DL

Dame Ditty, Melody and Tommy enter DR

Dame Y'now, findin' Tommy calls for a bit of a celebration!
Melody Yes. How about a picnic in the woods.
Dame (*to the audience*) Tch! Little Miss Rave up! (*To Melody*) I was thinkin' of goin' somewhere with *bar flies* not *blow flies*! Somewhere like the [local pub]!
Melody But we can't take the rest of the school there. They're too young.
Dame Oh, they can wait in the road and play with the traffic!
Tommy I think a picnic sounds like a jolly good idea.
Dame (*to the audience*) Tch! Another party pooper! Youngsters these days! They don't know how to enjoy themselves! (*To Tommy and Melody*) Oh, all right! A picnic it is! C'mon, let's go back to the 'ouse and sort out some grub. I think there's some sausage rolls left over from [long-past local event]!

Dame and Melody move to the exit DL

Tommy If you don't mind, I'll catch you up in a minute. I want to practise my scales.
Dame (*coming back, and slapping Tommy on the back*) Good lad! (*To the audience*) That's what I like to see! 'E's consi—conscien—consci—*keen*! (*To Tommy*) Melody'll come and get you when it's time to leave.

Dame and Melody exit DL

Tommy starts to practise scales

Discord creeps on from DL, *followed by Benny*

Discord (*aside to Benny*) Now's my chance to lure him away from old Ditty. (*He approaches Tommy*) Ah! Practice makes perfect, eh!
Tommy (*turning and seeing them*) Oh—hallo!
Discord (*smarmily*) You have a very fine voice, young man.
Tommy Thanks very much. (*He turns away, about to resume his scales*)
Discord (*with an exaggerated sigh*) Ahh! It really is a terrible shame.

Tommy What is?

Discord That such a magnificent voice as yours should be allowed to go to waste! It's a tragedy!

Tommy What do you mean?

Discord You have enrolled as a pupil at old ... er ... Dame Ditty's school, have you not?

Tommy Well—yes—I suppose I have.

Discord (*sighing deeply*) Ahh! A grave mistake!

Tommy Why?

Discord Because she is not qualified, young man, not qualified! *I*, on the other hand, am fully qualified to teach singing. I have the right credentials. Dr Discord, R.A.M.

Tommy What does that stand for?

Benny Rotten and mouldy!

Discord (*snarling at him*) Be quiet! (*Back to Tommy, very smarmily*) If you were to join *my* Academy, I would see to it that your talent was fully appreciated. I would have you singing at [local nightclub or theatre] in no time.

Tommy (*catching on to where this is leading*) I see. Well, say I did join you. You'd want me to sing in the contest this afternoon, I suppose?

Discord (*acting surprised*) What? The contest? Oh, dear me, I'd forgotten all about that—why, yes—you could.

Tommy This contest—I've been meaning to ask—is there a cash prize?

Discord A cash prize? Oh, no. There's nothing like that.

Benny Yes, there is! You remember! (*To Tommy*) It's a thousand pounds!

Discord (*jabbing Benny and snarling*) Idiot!!

Tommy A thousand pounds, eh? Tell me, if I did sing for you and won, what would be my share?

Discord Er ... your share? Er ... fifty pounds.

Tommy (*turning away, pretending to muse it over*) I see—and you get to keep the rest?

Discord (*trying to make light of it*) Well—yes—I do have certain expenses, and ...

Tommy (*turning on Discord, forcefully*) Well, Dr Discord, R.A.M.! Do you know what you can do with your fifty pounds? You can stick it up with your credentials! I already knew about the thousand pounds! Dame Ditty told me! She also told me that she was going to give me half of it! You weren't going to tell me about it at all, were you?! (*He advances, threateningly*)

Discord backs away and bumps into Benny. Both of them are flattened against the proscenium arch DL

> You're nothing but a low-down—conniving—cheating—underhanded old twister! And I wouldn't sing for you if your life depended on it!

Act I, Scene 2   23

Melody enters from DR

Melody What's going on?
Tommy (*moving to her*) Oh, it's nothing, Melody. That cheap chiseller was trying to poach me away from Dame Ditty, that's all. I told him where to get off.
Melody Good for you! We're ready to leave for the picnic now.
Tommy Right! (*He takes a threatening step towards Discord*)

Discord cowers back

Laughing, Tommy turns and exits DR

Venting his anger on Benny, Discord starts pushing him around. Melody rushes across

Melody Hey! Stop that! Don't take it out on him, just because your nasty little plan didn't work!
Discord (*pushing Benny aside and snarling at her*) I've got just one thing to say to *you*! (*Snarling at the audience*) And you!! Bah!! And—double bah!!

Snarling at the audience, Discord stomps out DR

Melody Are you all right, Benny?
Benny (*bashfully*) Yes, Melody.
Melody Are you in much pain?
Benny No—but my arm is.

She takes his arm and gently rubs it. This is ecstasy for Benny

Melody Is that better?

Benny just emits a blissful sigh

We're just going for a picnic in the woods. Would you like to come with us?
Benny (*delighted*) Oh, yes, please! (*Sadly*) But, I can't!
Melody Why not?
Benny I've gotta get back to Dr Discord's house. 'Is gutters need unblockin'.
Melody Why on earth do you work for that awful man? He treats you like dirt.
Benny (*sadly*) 'E owns our cottage. If I don't do as 'e says, 'e'll throw me an' my mum out.

Melody That's terrible! (*She takes his arm*) Oh, you poor thing.
Benny (*blissfully*) I am!
Melody You need a shoulder to cry on.
Benny (*putting his head on her shoulder*) I do!
Melody And someone to raise your self-esteem. (*She takes his hands*)
Benny You 'ave!

Song 7

A comedy duet and dance, making full use of Benny's bashful "love making"

Melody I'd better be going to the picnic. (*She moves to exit* DL, *then turns*) Goodbye, Benny. (*She blows him a kiss*)
Benny Goodbye, Melody. (*He makes a soppy attempt at blowing a kiss back*)

Melody exits DL

(*On cloud nine, hugging himself*) Oh, Melody—Melody! The name is like music to my ears! (*He waltzes about, blissfully humming the refrain on the duet*)

Discord enters from DR *and stands watching him with disgust*

Discord Benny!
Benny Comin', my darlin'! (*He waltzes across to Discord and realizes his mistake*) Ohh!
Discord (*bringing him forward, secretively*) Listen. I want you to go to the woods.
Benny (*overjoyed*) To Melody's nitpic... I mean, picnic?
Discord Certainly not! I want you to deliver a message for me! To Mother Curseum!
Benny (*backing away, scared*) M-Mother C-C-Curseum! Y-Y'mean that 'orrible old witch wot lives in the cave?
Discord The very same!
Benny B-B-But my mum says I shouldn't 'ave anythin' to do wiv 'er! She's a nasty piece o' work! Sh-She's in deague with the levil! I ain't goin' near 'er!
Discord (*grabbing him by the ear*) You'll do as I say, or you and your mother will be spending the night in the gutter! (*He twists his ear*) Understand!
Benny (*squirming with pain*) Ahhhow! Yes! Yes!
Discord (*releasing him*) Go and tell Mother Curseum I wish to consult her on a matter of extreme urgency. Say I will call upon her within the hour—with a purse of money! *That* should guarantee her full attention! Well, do as I say! Go!

Benny (*scared and trembling*) Ooooh!
Discord (*roaring*) Go!!

Benny runs out DR

(*To the audience, with a malevolent laugh*) Ha! Ha! Ha! With the help of Mother Curseum's magical powers, I am going to win that singing contest! And the thousand pounds! Oh, yes, I am! (*By-play with the audience*) And how am I going to do it? Well, you'll just have to wait and find out! But, do it, I shall! Ha! Ha! Ha!

Laughing and sneering at the audience, Discord exits DL, *as the Lights fade to Black-out*

Music to cover the scene change, then the Lights come up on——

Scene 3

The woods

Woodland backcloth with foliage groundrow. Tree and foliage side wings. An overgrown cave entrance UR. *A clump of bushes* UL. *A large picnic hamper* UC. *On the ground, near it, a cloth covered with the remains of the picnic. Bright, sunny Lighting*

Discovered—the Chorus are grouped at the back and sides, either standing or seated on the ground. Dame Ditty and the Duke are sitting on the hamper. Tommy and Sophie are together, R. *Melody and the group of Girl Pupils,* L

Song 8

This can be a singing number involving the Principals and Chorus, or a speciality dance for the Dancers, or a pleasant combination of the two

Dame (*rising*) It was lovely of you to join our picnic, your Dukefulness.
Duke (*rising*) It was lovely of *you* to ask us, Dame Ditty. Sophie and I only came into these woods for a quick constitutional.
Dame Oh? 'Aven't you got one in the Manor 'ouse then? Are you sure I can't press you to somethin' else? (*She sidles up close to him*) A couple of my flapjacks, per'aps?
Duke Thankee, no. I've had quite sufficient. (*Patting his belly*) I'm carryin' far too much weight as it is!

Dame Nonsense! You're like me—big-boned.

During the following dialogue, the Chorus and Pupils collect up the picnic things, put them in the hamper, and exit with it

Sophie (*to all, as if making a casual remark, but we guess it's just a ruse to be alone with Tommy*) These woods are truly enchanting. I should very much like to explore them further.
Tommy (*catching on*) Yes—so should I.
Sophie Really? Then why don't we explore them together?
Tommy What a splendid idea! (*Offering his arm*) Allow me.
Sophie (*taking his arm*) Thank you.

The young couple move towards the exit R

Duke Sophie, m'dear! That young man is a competitor in the contest. And as *we're* puttin' up the prize money, and as *you* pointed out to *me* earlier, I don't think we should be showin' any favouritism.
Sophie (*disappointed, but conceding*) Yes … you're quite right, Papa. (*To Tommy, releasing his arm*) I'm sorry.
Tommy (*aside to her*) Not half as sorry as I am! (*He slouches out,* R)

Dame Ditty looks around and sees that the Chorus, etc., have gone. She is obviously eager to be alone with the Duke

Dame Melody, dear! Why don't *you* take Miss Sophie to see the rest of the woods?
Melody I'd be delighted. (*She moves to exit* L) This way.
Sophie (*crossing to her*) Thank you. (*She turns*) Will you not join us, Papa?
Dame (*leaping in*) No!! (*Controlling herself*) Er… Per'aps the Dukey wants a rest. 'E can stay 'ere with me for a little chat. A little tatty-tate! (*She gives him a nudge and a wink*)
Duke (*wavering*) Well… I … er…
Sophie (*smiling*) Remember, Papa—no favouritism.
Duke What? By Jove, yes! Quite right, m'dear! (*To Melody*) Lead on!

Melody, Sophie and the Duke exit L

Dame (*to the audience*) Oh, drat!! And I wanted to get 'im on 'is own, girls! (*Struck by an idea*) I know! (*She goes to the exit* L, *and calls loudly*) Help!! Save me!! Help!! Oooh!! Help!! Save me!! (*She looks off, then gives the audience the thumbs up*) 'E's comin' back! (*She rushes* C, *and pretends to be warding off a bee*)

Act I, Scene 3   27

The Duke rushes on from L

Duke (*concerned*) Egad! Dame Ditty! What's the matter?!
Dame (*rushing to him in a panic*) It's a bee!! A great big bumble bee!! (*She throws her arms around him, the "panic" over*) I think it's buzzed off now! Thanks to you! My hero! (*She flutters her eyelashes, coyly*)
Duke (*flustered, and not knowing what else to say*) Er ... yes ... I must say this is a very charming spot.
Dame Oh, thank you! Do you like it? I've got one on my other cheek too! (*She turns her face*) Look!
Duke I was referrin' to this part of the wood. It's so peaceful and quiet.

A loud peal of maniacal, cackling laughter echoes from the cave! (On an offstage microphone)

Zounds! What the deuce was that?! (*He moves towards the cave*)

Anxious that they should not be interrupted, Dame Ditty follows, still clinging to his arm

Dame Oh, don't worry about it, Dukey! I expect it was just a bird!
Duke A *bird*, Madam! I should hate to meet the bird who makes a noise like that! (*Concerned*) I hope it didn't distress you too much, dear lady?
Dame (*dismissively*) Nah! (*She realizes she can use this to her advantage*) Oh—well—as a matter of fact—it did give me rather a nasty turn! Yes! Oooh! I feel most peculiar! Oooh! (*She staggers away, pretending to feel faint*) I... I *think* I'm goin' to faint! (*She gives him a look, then staggers a bit further*) Oooh! Yes! I'm *definitely* goin' to faint! (*She looks back to see he hasn't moved*) I said—(*very loudly*) I'm goin' to faint!

The Duke rushes across and she collapses into his arms

Duke (*staggering under her weight*) D-Dame Ditty! Are you all right?
Dame (*hauling herself up on him*) Oooh! Ooow! (*She puts her hand to her forehead*) Oh, it's the vapours! The vapours! Hold me! Hold me!

He tentatively puts his arms around her waist

Tighter than that!! (*She hugs him, very tightly. To the audience*) I think I've pulled, girls!
Duke (*hardly able to breathe, going weak at the knees*) Are—you—feeling—better?
Dame Oh, yes! Don't drop me, that's all! (*She is in fact holding him up*) Oh,

Dukey, whatever would people say if they found us in this compromising position?
Duke (*able only to let out a groan*) Urrragh!
Dame Exactly! Well, let them say what they like! I don't care, if you don't care!

Song 9

A comically "seductive" song and dance, in which Dame Ditty is very physical in showing her "passion", and the poor Duke is a helpless "rag doll". The number ends with her bending him over in a "passionate" embrace, then letting him fall to the ground

(*To the audience, elated*) Oh, girls! I think 'e's fallen for me in a big way!

On his hands and knees, the Duke makes his escape off L

Dukey, darlin'! Come back! I 'aven't finished with you yet!

Dame runs out after him, calling

(*Off*) Dukey! Come to Ditty! Dukey!

As soon as her voice dies away, there is another peal of fiendish laughter from the cave (Offstage microphone). At the same time, the Lighting becomes dark and sinister

Discord creeps on from DR. *He reaches back into the wings, and drags on a trembling and terrified Benny*

Discord (*to the audience, with his evil laugh*) Ha! Ha! Ha! Ha! Still here, are you? Good! For now you will see how I plan to win the contest! (*To Benny, pulling him forward*) What did the witch say when you told her I wished to speak with her?
Benny Not much. She said it'd be all right, and told me to clear off or she'd turn me into a ... into a... (*he shivers with disgust*) no, it's too 'orrible to repeat!
Discord Turn you into a what?
Benny A [local football team] supporter!
Discord (*grimacing*) Egh! That *is* horrible! Well, let's call her out. Where is the cave?
Benny (*nervously leading Discord up to the cave entrance*) It's 'ere! There's a bell.

Act I, Scene 3   29

Discord Then ring it, dummy!

Reluctantly, Benny uncovers a bell push near the cave mouth. He presses it. Eerie organ music is heard inside the cave. Both react, then Discord gestures for Benny to try again. He presses the bell, and the organ music is heard again

Benny She's probably gone shoppin' at Tesco's [or local store]! Let's go 'ome!
Discord (*pushing him back*) No! Try again!

Benny presses the bell. This time all hell breaks loose! Thunder and lightning! Howling winds! Uncanny wails and laughter! Weird lights flash across the stage, and a strange mist billows from the cave. Benny and Discord back away in terror. The sounds gradually fade away. The Lighting remains dark and sinister

To suitably "devilish" music, a band of grotesque Goblins, Imps and Demons emerge from the cave. They prance about, performing a short, weird dance

Song 10: Demon Dance

After the dance, the Demons, etc., gather around the cave entrance and fall to their knees

There is a blinding flash of lightning and a great roll of thunder. An eerie green spotlight illuminates the cave mouth, and more mist billows out. The Demons, etc., bow their heads in homage

From out of the mist appears the repulsive figure of Mother Curseum, the witch. She raises her arms and gives a fiendish cackle. This develops into a coughing fit as she inhales some of the mist! Coughing and spluttering, she comes out, waving the mist away

Curseum Phew! I'll have to get that new cauldron looked at! (*She sees Discord and Benny and adopts a characteristic stance and voice*)
            I am Mother Curseum, the queen of witches!
            Black magic performed without any hitches!
            My powers are great and truly amazing!
            I hope you're not here to flog double glazing!

Discord moves to Curseum. Benny keeps his distance. Take out spotlight on Curseum

Discord Mother Curseum, how do you do. I sent a message that I wanted to consult you. I am Dr Discord, R.A.M.
Curseum What's that stand for?
Benny Rotten and mouldy!
Discord (*snarling at him*) Be quiet!
Curseum (*indicating the audience*) And why have you brought *this lot* with you? (*She scrutinises the audience*) Who are they? What do they want?
Discord Oh, take no notice of that rabble! (*He sneers at the audience*)
Curseum I shan't! And if they give me any trouble, I'll turn them all into pigs! Oh, sorry! Somebody's already done that! (*To Discord, curtly*) Well? What is it you want? I'm up to my eyes this mornin'! I've got three broomsticks in for repair, and there's twenty wax effigies of [politician] that need pins stickin' in! Make it quick!
Discord Certainly. At the local fair this afternoon they are holding a singing contest, and...
Curseum (*irritably*) Yes, yes, I know all about that! The singer's got to be male an' the winner gets a thousand pounds. Dame Ditty's got young Tommy Tucker, an' you're stuck with wailing Willie, over there.
Discord That's amazing! I suppose you read it in the runes?
Curseum No—the [local newspaper]! Get on with it!
Discord I must win that contest! My whole reputation as a music teacher depends on it.
Curseum (*sarcastically*) And, of course, you've got no interest in the thousand pounds! Well, what d'you want me to do?
Discord I want you to remove Tommy Tucker's singing voice and transfer it to *him*! (*He points to Benny*)

Benny reacts

Can you do that?
Curseum (*indignantly*) Can I do that, he asks! No trouble. I once transferred a brain to [topical "dim" personality]! How much? That sort of magic doesn't come cheap, y'know.
Discord I'll pay you—a hundred pounds.
Curseum (*scoffing*) A hundred pounds! Leapin' Lucifer! That ain't worth dirtyin' a cauldron for! Two hundred pounds! Take it or leave it!
Discord (*grudgingly*) Oh, very well! Will a cheque suit you?
Curseum Not with my colourin'! (*She thrusts out her hand*) Cash!

Grumbling to himself, Discord takes out a wallet and gives her notes. Putting the money down the front of her dress, (or some other amusing hiding place!) Curseum goes up to the cave entrance

Act I, Scene 3

(*Calling inside*) Primrose! Primrose, bring out the number two cauldron, an' the box of tricks! (*She moves back to Discord*)

Benny (*nervously*) I... I think I'll be g-g-goin' 'ome now... (*He makes for the exit*)

Discord pulls him back

From out of the cave comes Primrose, pushing a "smoking" cauldron on wheels. Under her arm is a black box covered with magic symbols. Primrose is a very odd-looking individual. Hardly human, in fact! She wheels the cauldron over and parks it in front of Curseum

Curseum This is Primrose, my charmin' young assistant.

Primrose does a twirl like a conjuror's assistant. It's clumsy, to say the least

She used to be a model for Vivienne Westwood, y'know. Now to make up the magic potion. Primrose—the box!

Primrose holds the box open

(*Looking in the box*) Now. Let's see. What do I need for this one? (*As she recites, she takes various items from the box and either throws them into the cauldron or out into the audience. Note: the items thrown at the audience are made from sweets*)
        Entrails of cat—Yes! (*Cauldron*)
        Eyeballs of rat—No! (*Audience*)
        Fleas of dog—Yes! (*Cauldron*)
        Tongues of frog—No! (*Audience*)
        Rotten fruit—Yes! (*Cauldron*)
        Eyes of newt—No! (*Audience*)
        Widdecombe's hair—Yes! (*Cauldron*)
        Teeth of Blair—No! (*Audience*)
        Beetles and bugs—Yes! (*Cauldron*)
        Slimy slugs...
Oh! Slimy slugs? Now, I wonder if...? (*She ponders, weighing the "slugs" in her hand, and making the audience feel uneasy. Finally, she is about to throw them into the cauldron, but at the last moment, throws them into the audience, with a fiendish cackle*) Hee! Hee! Hee! (*To the audience*) Accordin' to Delia, they're delicious with a little crème fraîche. (*Back to work*) Just add a pinch of salt! (*She tosses a whole box of salt into the cauldron*) Give it a good stir!

Primrose hands her a long wooden spoon

(*Stirring*) And allow to simmer, while casting the magic spell! (*She raises her arms and gives a fiendish cackle*) Hee! Hee! Hee! Hee!

The lighting becomes even more dark and sinister. An evil, green spotlight illuminates Curseum and the cauldron area. Menacing music plays under. The Demons, etc., crawl over and kneel in front of the cauldron. They move their arms as Curseum casts the spell

Curseum (*making magic passes over the cauldron*)
Hubble, grubble and cauldron bubble!
Gurgle and burble like toilet trouble!
O, powers of darkness hark to me,
And aid my work in sorcery!
Infuse this potion, and I'll rejoice!
Make it steal Tommy Tucker's voice!

She makes a final, dramatic pass at the cauldron, and gives an even more fiendish cackle

Ha! Ha! Hee! Hee! Hee!

There is a blinding flash and puff of smoke from (or near) the cauldron. All hell breaks loose again! Thunder and lightning! Flashing lights and howling winds, etc., etc.! The Demons jabber in devilish delight. Benny clings to Discord, trembling with fear. Finally, Curseum calls a halt to the upheaval

Cut!!

All the noises and flashing lights, etc., stop abruptly. The sinister Lighting and spotlight remain. Cursem takes an empty bottle from the box and dips it into the cauldron. When she brings it out, it is full of bright green liquid (duplicate bottle already in cauldron). She holds the bottle up and gives a triumphant cackle

Hee! Hee! Hee! Behold—the magic potion!

The Demons, etc., jibber and jabber, excitedly. The spotlight fades out, and the general lighting becomes a little brighter

(*To Demons*) All right! All right! Get back to yer work!

The Demons, etc., scuttle away into the cave

Act I, Scene 3

Primrose, take the cauldron away and stick it in the dishwasher.

Primrose gives a grunt and wheels the cauldron into the cave

Curseum holds up the bottle and admires it

Not a bad drop of potion that, even if I do say so meself. (*She holds it out to Discord*) Here ya go!
Discord (*taking it*) But—what do I do with it?
Curseum What d'you think you do with it—clean the loo? You get Tommy Tucker to drink it, of course. (*Aside to the audience*) How thick can you get!
Discord But how? He'll never accept a drink from *me*! He'll be suspicious. Listen—suppose *you* get him to drink it.
Curseum And you don't think *I'm* suspicious?
Discord Not as yourself. As someone he trusts.
Curseum Are you askin' me to change myself into someone else?
Discord Exactly!
Curseum (*mulling it over*) Mmm. I ain't done that for ages. Not since the landlord came lookin' for his rent. Right, you're on. Who do you want me to be? Who does he trust?
Discord How about that old trout, Dame Ditty?
Curseum (*grimacing*) No, ta! Even *I've* got standards!
Discord How about her pupil then—Melody?
Curseum (*thinking it over, then shaking her head*) Nah... (*Struck by an idea*) Here! What about that young woman who was at the picnic with her highfaloopin' father? Tommy Tucker seemed very keen on her.
Discord You must mean the Duke of Sterling's daughter, Sophie! Yes! Perfect! Change yourself into her!
Curseum At least I'll get to wear an expensive frock! Right! Here goes then! (*She moves away to near* DR *wing*)

The Lighting becomes darker. Mysterious music plays under. An eerie spotlight on Curseum as she casts the spell

(*Raising her arms*) O, powers of darkness hark to me.
        And aid my work in sorcery!
        Work your charms just like you oughter,
        And change me into the Duke's fair daughter!

There is a blinding flash, followed by a complete Black-out. When the Lights come up, (returning to bright sunshine effect) we see that the transformation has been a complete success. Curseum has become Sophie! Although she looks and sounds like that beautiful young lady, the witch still retains her own mannerisms and inflexions. She examines herself with delight and gives a triumphant cackle

Sophie Hee! Hee! Hee! (*She goes to Discord and Benny*) What d'you think? (*She does a twirl*) Not bad, eh?
Discord (*genuinely impressed*) It's amazing—amazing!
Sophie I dunno why I ain't done this before! I'd be a lot more popular.

Tommy is heard singing, off DR, *an unaccompanied refrain of Song 5*

Discord Listen! That sounds like Tommy Tucker now! (*He looks off* R) Yes! He's coming this way! Here! (*He gives her the bottle*)
Sophie Leave him to me! (*With a fiendish cackle*) Hee! Hee! Hee!

Discord goes up and hides behind the clump of bushes, L. *Benny hovers, still amazed by the fake Sophie. Discord comes back and drags him behind the bushes. We can just see the tops of their heads as they crouch, watching the proceedings. Meanwhile, the witch gets into character and adopts a perfect imitation of Sophie's demure stance and manner. She holds the bottle behind her back*

Still singing, Tommy strolls on from DR. *He breaks off when he sees Sophie standing there*

Tommy Oh! Hallo, Sophie.
Sophie Hallo, Tommy.
Tommy (*looking about*) All on your own?
Sophie Yes.
Tommy (*moving to her, with open arms*) Not any more!
Sophie (*taking a step back*) If you don't mind me saying so, you're a little hoarse.
Tommy Na—ay! (*He laughs at his "joke"*)
Sophie (*aside*) Plonker! (*To Tommy*) Your voice sounds rather husky.
Tommy (*surprised*) Does it?
Sophie Yes, very.
Tommy It's probably all this singing practice.
Sophie Yes. I expect you'd like a *nice cold* drink.
Tommy I wouldn't say no.
Sophie Then I've got just what you need. (*She produces the bottle*) Try this! (*She holds the bottle out to him*)
Tommy (*taking it*) Thanks. What an odd colour! Is it Robinson's? (*He removes the bottle top*)
Sophie Yes! (*Aside*) Anne Robinson's! Hee! Hee!

Act I, Scene 3   35

Tommy (*sniffing and reacting*) Cor! Phew! It's got a very peculiar smell! Are you sure it's all right to drink?
Sophie It's perfectly all right. It's delicious. Try some.
Tommy (*dubiously*) I... I don't know... (*To the audience*) Do you think I should, folks?

"No!!" from the audience

Sophie (*to the audience, still demure*) Oh, yes, he should.

"Oh, no, he shouldn't!"/"Oh, yes, he should!" routine with the audience follows. As it progresses, the fake Sophie forgets herself and the aggression of Curseum takes over

Tommy (*puzzled by the change in her*) Sophie—are you all right?
Sophie (*returning to character*) Yes ... yes. It's just that—if you don't trust me, Tommy... (*She turns away, pretending to be hurt and upset*) Anyone would think I was trying to poison you...
Tommy (*rushing to her*) Of course I trust you, Sophie. And to prove it—look! (*He drinks from the bottle*)

As he is doing so, Sophie turns away to give Discord the thumbs up

(*Lowering the bottle and pleasantly surprised*) Mmm! It *is* good! Very nice. (*He replaces the top and hands her the bottle*) Thank you. It tastes a bit like... (*But he says no more! He is suddenly frozen. He stands, facing front, in a hypnotic trance*)
Sophie (*cackling with devilish glee*) Hee! Hee! Hee! (*To Discord*) Quick! Bring him out!

Discord drags Benny out, as Sophie turns the frozen Tommy to face sideways. She grabs Benny and positions him so that he is facing Tommy

Now to transfer the singing voice!
Benny (*quacking*) Ooooow!!
Sophie Don't worry. It doesn't hurt—much! Not half as painful as watchin' "Big Brother"! Hee! Hee! Hee!

The Lighting becomes dark and sinister again. An eerie spotlight on Tommy and Benny. Mysterious music plays under as Sophie casts the spell

(*Raising her arms*) O, powers of darkness hark to me,
      And aid my work in sorcery!

>   The golden voice of Tommy Tucker,
>   Now transfer to this silly sucker! (*She makes a magic pass at the couple*)

With an involuntary action, both Tommy and Benny open their mouths wide. Strange, tinkling sounds are heard, suggesting the voice transference. Tommy shuts his mouth. Benny starts coughing and spluttering. He clutches his throat, then gives a huge swallow. The tinkling sounds fade away. The Lighting returns to bright sunshine effect

Discord (*eagerly*) Well? Has it worked?
Sophie (*poking Benny*) Go on—sing!
Benny Eh?
Sophie \
Discord / (*together; snarling at him*) Sing!

Nervous and bewildered, Benny clears his throat and sings. It is a very pleasant sound indeed! (Unaccompanied refrain of Song 7.) He is at once puzzled, amazed and delighted by the glorious sound coming from his own throat

Discord (*while Benny is still singing*) Excellent! Excellent! (*To Benny loudly*) You can shut up now!

Benny stops singing, but continues to mime, obviously overjoyed by his new-found talent. Tommy remains frozen

>   (*To Sophie, indicating Tommy*) What about him?
> **Sophie** Oh, he'll wake up in a minute, not knowin' anythin's happened! (*With evil relish*) Until he tries to sing, that is!

Discord and Sophie laugh at the audience with sneering laughs

Discord \ (*together*) Ha! Ha! Ha!
Sophie /   Hee! Hee! Hee!
Sophie Well, that's my bit done! (*She moves up to the cave*) I'd better get changed back, or Primrose an' the others'll get confused. Shame really. Still, all in a day's devilment! Hee! Hee! Hee!

Sophie exits into the cave

Benny starts singing aloud again. He now accompanies it with his idea of grand, expressive gestures

Discord (*going to Benny*) All right! All right! (*He clamps his hand over Benny's mouth*) Don't waste it! (*He pushes Benny away to* R. *With disgust, he wipes his hand on Benny's sleeve*)

The Duke and Dame Ditty enter from L. *She clings to his arm. He is looking very hot and bothered, and is mopping his face with a handkerchief*

Dame You shouldn't keep tryin' to run away from me, Dukey, then you wouldn't get so 'ot and bothered! (*She sees Discord and Benny*) Oh, look! It's old Discord and Charles Aznovoice! Ha! Ha! Ha!
Discord (*joining in with her laughter*) Ha! Ha! Ha!
Dame I don't know what *you've* got to laugh about, Mr Loser! I'm all set to win that contest!
Discord (*to the audience, with a sneering laugh*) Ha! Ha! That's what *she* thinks!
Dame (*going to the still frozen Tommy*) Isn't that right, Tommy? (*She sees his condition and reacts*) Tommy...? What's up wi' 'im...? Stop day dreamin'! (*She prods him*) Tommy! Wake up!
Tommy (*suddenly coming back to life, and carrying on the conversation where he left off*) ...Lime juice. (*He sees the Dame standing there and is rather confused*) Oh! Dame Ditty—I... I'm sorry—I thought you were Sophie. (*He looks about, puzzled*)
Dame An easy mistake to make!
Duke (*moving over*) Where is my daughter? We really must be getting back to the Manor. (*He mops his brow*) I need to lie down and rest.
Dame (*flitting down to him, and clinging to his arm*) Why don't you come back to my place, Dukey? You can lie down there, but I can't guarantee you'll get much rest! (*She winks and nudges him*)

Sophie (the real one) enters from L, *with Melody*

Half of the Chorus and the Girl Pupils enter UL

Very relieved, the Duke crosses to Sophie. During the following, Tommy moves down stage

Duke Ah, Sophie! There you are, thank goodness! It's time we were goin', m'dear. Come along. (*He hastily leads her towards the exit* DR)
Sophie (*to the Others, as she goes*) Goodbye... (*To Tommy*) Goodbye, Tommy.
Tommy Goodbye, and thanks for the drink.
Sophie Drink? What...

But the Duke has led her away, and off DR

Discord (*to Dame, with a crafty smirk*) I'm really looking forward to the singing contest, aren't you?
Dame *I* am, yes! But I don't know why you are! You don't stand a chance with tone deaf Tinkerbell, over there!

Laughter from the Chorus and Pupils

Discord Ah, but that's just where you're wrong. Under my expert tutelage he has improved enormously.
Dame (*sarcastically*) Oh, look! There's a pig flyin' over!

More laughter from the others

Discord (*to Benny*) Show them your prowess.
Benny (*dumbly*) My wot?
Discord Sing!

Benny steps forward and clears his throat. Preparing for the worst, the Dame and the Chorus put their fingers in their ears. Benny opens his mouth and sings. Again, the glorious sound issues forth! General sensation! Dame Ditty and the others remove their fingers, and gape at Benny in amazement and disbelief. He finishes singing and takes a bow. Tommy, Melody and the others applaud him. Dame Ditty is too gobsmacked to do anything

(*To Dame, smirking*) What do you say now?
Dame (*flummoxed*) I ... I ... er! Well ... er—'e's a little better... (*Brightening*) but 'e's still not a patch on our Tommy! (*She pulls Tommy forward*) Go on, Tommy! Give 'em a blast of the really good stuff!

Tommy clears his throat and sings. An atrocious noise comes out! General sensation! The most surprised and shocked is Tommy himself. He makes a second attempt, but it's worse than the first. Dame Ditty is even more gobsmacked than before. Discord bursts into mocking laughter

Discord Ha! Ha! Ha! Oh, dear, dear, dear! (*To Dame*) It looks like your song bird has developed the croup! Ha! Ha! Ha!

Dame and Melody rush to the bewildered Tommy

Melody Tommy! What's happened to your voice?
Tommy I ... I don't know—I ... I just can't seem to—I can't sing any more!

Discord roars with mocking laughter

Act I, Scene 3

Dame (*in a flap*) Ooh! Crumple me crochets! What are we gonna do! Quick! Let's get 'im 'ome an' try a throat spray!

Discord (*viciously*) Try what you like, you old trout! *He's* finished! *You're* finished! I'm going to win that singing contest now! And the thousand pounds! Ha! Ha! Ha!

Discord continues to laugh, as Dame Ditty and Melody lead the bemused Tommy out L

The Chorus and the Pupils follow them out

The Lighting becomes dark and sinister. An "evil" spotlight on Discord, as he turns to address the audience

Ha! Ha! Ha! You see! I told you I had a plan! And it worked! Tommy Tucker is finished! He will never sing again! The prize is mine! All mine! Ha! Ha! Ha! (*He grabs Benny*) Come along, my little canary! Ha! Ha! Ha!

Still laughing his evil laugh, Discord drags Benny out DL. *Just as they exit, Curseum (now back to abnormal!) comes out of the cave. The "evil" spotlight transfers to her. She is followed by Primrose and the little Demons, etc.*

Curseum (*to the audience*) Hee! Hee! Hee! That's what I like to see—a satisfied customer! Primrose, this calls for a celebration! Let's give them hell! Hee! Hee! Hee!

All hell breaks loose yet again. Thunder and lightning! Howling winds! Uncanny noises, etc., etc.! Red, flickering lights fill the stage and ground mist swirls in from the sides

The other half of the Chorus and the Dancers enter the scene, as Ghouls, Zombies and other Grotesque Monsters from the Netherworld

Song 11

A wild display of demonic singing and dancing by the Chorus and Dancers. Curseum and Primrose comically cavort and dance together. The number ends with Curseum leaping into Primrose's arms, and the Chorus grouped around them, as——

—*the* CURTAIN *falls*

ACT II

Scene 1

Dame Ditty's garden

Prominent L is the back of Dame Ditty's house, with a practical door. Across the back runs a low fence, broken in the centre by a gate or opening. The backcloth shows countryside with the fairground in the middle distance. Tree, flowers and foliage side wings

When the CURTAIN *rises, Melody is discovered giving the Girl Pupils a lesson in singing and dancing. The Chorus and Dancers are grouped at the sides and outside the fence. They also participate in the musical number*

Song 12

Melody Thank you, class. That'll be all for today. I'm sure you're all eager to go home and get ready for the fair.

Some of the Chorus collect their various offspring

Woman (*to Melody*) Have you had any luck in getting Tommy Tucker his voice back?
Melody Not yet. Dame Ditty's in the house now, trying out different throat sprays on him.

At this point, Tommy's atrocious attempts at singing are heard coming from the house. The Chorus and Children cringe and react

Woman Without much success by the sound of it! Let's hope she finds a remedy, or Discord's going to win the singing contest. It's in less than an hour's time, y'know.
Melody (*trying to make light of it*) Oh, I'm sure he's going to be all right. It's just a technical hitch.

More atrocious noises from Tommy are heard!

Reacting, the Chorus and Children exit UC

Act II, Scene 1 41

Dame Ditty comes out of her house, followed by Tommy. Both are looking very downcast

Any luck?
Dame Not a sausage! I've sprayed 'is throat with everythin' I can find! I even tried Mr Sheen! No good, but 'e's got a lovely shine on 'is tongue! Look!

Tommy sticks his tongue out

You can see yer face in it! (*To the audience*) Don't try it at 'ome, kids! (*To Tommy*) You can put it away now!

Tommy does so

I don't know what else to try! (*To the audience*) 'Ave you got any ideas, folks? (*Ad lib and by play with the audience. Then to Melody, desperately*) Oh, what are we gonna do! The contest's in an hour! (*To Tommy*) Oh, 'ow could you lose yer voice at a time like this!
Tommy (*shrugging, hopelessly*) I wish I knew!
Melody Perhaps it's psychological.
Dame Yes. (*With a double take*) Cyclin*what*ical?!
Melody Perhaps it's all in his mind. Deep down Tommy has a fear of singing in public.
Tommy I haven't!
Melody Ah, that's what you think. But in your subconscious you have. And part of your brain has shut down your ability to sing.
Dame (*to the audience*) I 'ope you lot are followin' this! That's what you get for sendin' ' em to [local school or college]! (*To Melody*) All right! Suppose it is this cyclin' thing—what can we do about it?
Melody We must help him to overcome his fear.
Tommy But, I'm not afraid of——
Dame Be quiet while the doctor's talkin'! (*To Melody*) Go on.
Melody We need to encourage him to sing in front of a lot of people.
Dame Anythin's worth a try! (*She indicates the audience*) And we've got a lot of people sat sittin' 'ere doin' nothin'! (*To the audience*) You'll 'elp us, won't you, folks?

"Yes!" from the audience

Tommy (*mildly protesting*) But, I didn't think——
Dame Be quiet! We're goin' to sort out your sub ... sub ... subsidence, or whatever it's called.
Melody Now, we'll try a simple song to begin with. Something like ... er ...

The pianist/band plays the tune of the chosen number. A song that everyone will know

Yes! That will do perfectly. (*To the audience*) You all know that one. Now, when it's Tommy's turn to sing, you all sing with him and help him out. Got that? Good!

Song 13

Melody and Dame Ditty start the singing, then encourage Tommy and the audience to join in. He sounds even more off-key and atrocious! The whole thing goes from bad to worse, and finally Dame Ditty calls a halt to it

Dame Wow!! Wow! All right! Forget it! Forget it! Thanks for your 'elp, folks, but it's not workin', is it? I don't know whether *he's* puttin' *you* off, or the other way around! (*To Melody, sarcastically*) Any more ideas, Dr Freud!

Benny runs on from DR

Benny (*gasping*) Melody...! Dame Ditty...! (*He bends over to catch his breath*)
Dame Oh, look! It's Placebo Domingo! I suppose old Discord's sent you 'ere to gloat!
Benny No! 'E doesn't know I'm 'ere! I... I...
Melody Calm down, Benny, and tell us what's wrong.
Benny I... I know why Tommy can't sing any more ... it's because——
Duke (*off* UR; *calling*) Dame Ditty! Dame Ditty!

The Duke enters at the back and comes straight down. He is followed by Sophie and the sniffing Boy

Dame Ditty! (*He sees her*) Ah! There you are!
Dame Oh, hallo, Dukey! What's up? Can't bear to let me out of your sight, eh? (*She winks and nudges him*)
Duke I've just heard some very disturbin' news!
Dame Oh, don't tell me they're gonna do another series of [TV flop]?!
Duke I have just been informed that your contestant, Tommy Tucker, has lost his ability to sing! Is this true?
Dame (*flustered*) Well, I... I...
Sophie Is it true, Tommy?
Tommy (*about to admit the truth*) I'm afraid it——
Dame (*leaping in*) No! No! No! 'Course it's not true! (*To Duke*) Where on earth did you hear that load of old codswallop?

Duke (*bringing the Boy forward*) From this young fellow.
Boy S'right! (*Sniff*)
Dame Oh, *him*! (*She pretends to laugh it off*) Ha! Ha! Oh, you don't want to listen to anythin' 'e says, Dukey!
Boy But it's true! Everyone knows——

Dame Ditty clamps her hand over the Boy's mouth, and pretends to cuddle him

Dame Oo! 'E's a sweet little chap! But 'e does like tellin' porkie pies! Don't you?

The Boy struggles

Yes! (*She drags him towards the exit* DL) Now, run along and play, my little cherub! (*Aside to Boy, showing him her fist*) An' don't come back, if you know what's good for ya! (*With a kick in the pants, she propels the Boy off* DL. *Comic business as she wipes her hand on the main tabs*)
Duke So, there is no truth in it?
Dame Certainly not! It's just a ... a thingamy of lies.
Duke A tissue?
Dame Bless you!
Duke But that boy seemed so certain.
Sophie Papa, if it still troubles you, why don't you ask Tommy to sing for you—right now.

Horrified reaction from Dame Ditty and Melody. Quickly, Benny takes Tommy to one side and whispers to him

Duke Of course! M'dear! Good thinkin'. That'll settle it.
Dame (*in a panic*) He can't!
Duke Why not?
Dame (*slumped*) Why not? (*To Melody*) Why not?
Melody (*thinking fast*) Because—we don't want him to strain his vocal chords just before the contest.
Dame That's it! 'E mustn't stain 'is cocal vords ... 'is local mords ... 'is... (*She gives up*) Oh, what she said!

Benny quickly hides behind a tree R

Duke But surely it can't hurt to...
Tommy It's all right, your Grace. I'm quite happy to sing for you.
Dame (*turning away with an agonized groan*) Ooh, no!!
Duke (*to Tommy*) Pray proceed.

Tommy goes and stands in front of the tree behind which Benny is hiding. At C, the Duke and Sophie turn to face him. Fearing the worst, Dame Ditty and Melody tip-toe away, towards the DL exit. Tommy clears his throat, and sings. A marvellous sound issues forth! It is, in fact, Benny singing and Tommy miming. Dame Ditty and Melody stop in their tracks, and turn round. They comprehend the deception. The Duke and Sophie are puzzled. Something doesn't sound right, but what is it? Tommy finishes "singing" and takes a bow. Dame Ditty and Melody applaud loudly

Dame Y'see! 'E's as good as ever!
Duke (*still puzzled*) Well—that proves he can still sing—but ... er ... his voice seems to have changed somewhat.
Sophie (*to Tommy*) Yes. It certainly does sound different.
Dame (*leaping in*) Well, that's our Tommy for ya! Hidden talents!
Duke Er ... yes ... well, I am glad to see there is nothing amiss. I should have hated to see you without your competitor.
Dame (*nudging him*) Oh, you cheeky thing, you! I bet you say that to all the girls!
Duke Come, Sophie. Let us return home and dress for the fair. (*To the others*) See you all at the contest.

The Duke and Sophie exit UC

As soon as they are out of sight, Tommy brings Benny from behind the tree

Tommy (*shaking his hand*) Well done, Benny! Thanks very much!
Dame Yes! You certainly saved our bacon.
Melody You were about to tell us why Tommy can't sing any more.
Benny It's magic!
Others Magic?
Benny Yeah! Dr Discord got that old witch, Mother Curseum, to do it! She made a magic portion!
Others Potion!
Benny Yeah! That an' all! Then she changed 'erself into Miss Sophie an' got Tommy to drink it!
Tommy You mean—it wasn't really Sophie who gave me that drink?
Dame (*to Tommy*) Oh, keep up! Keep up! (*To Benny*) Go on!
Benny Then Tommy went into a dance!
Others What?!
Benny I ... I mean—a trance! Then the witch made an awful smell ... er ... spell, an' Tommy's voice sort of came into me! Thas why I'm a good singer now!
Dame (*scoffing*) You're 'avin' us on! That's even more far-fetched than [TV soap or film].

Act II, Scene 1   45

Benny It's true! (*To the audience*) *You* saw it 'appen, didn't you, folks?

"Yes!" from the audience

Dame (*getting her dander up*) Oo! That rotten Discord! 'E's a rotten old rotter!
Melody What are we going to do?
Tommy We've got to find someone with magic powers who can break the spell.
Dame But who? Old Mother Curseum's the only witch in town! Not like at [local place]! (*To the audience*) I'm told there's lots of old witches there! (*To the others, despairingly*) Oh, let's face it, gang! We're sunk! We can't fight magic!
Melody Wait a minute! The other day someone told me that a man had just moved into Rosebud Cottage. He had with him a lot of strange-looking boxes and things.
Dame So what? 'E's probably on the inter web—or outer net—or whatever it's called.
Melody Some of the boxes had magical symbols and signs painted on them. Perhaps he's a magician.
Dame Well, don't just stand there, girl! Run and fetch 'im!

Melody runs out DL

Discord enters from DR

Discord (*seeing Benny*) So! This is where you're hiding! (*He crosses and grabs Benny by the ear*) I told you not to leave my house until it was time for the singing contest! (*Twisting Benny's ear, he drags him to the* DR *exit*)

Tommy rushes across and forces Discord to release Benny

Tommy Leave him alone!
Dame Yes, you connivin' old creep, you! We know all about your nasty little game! Usin' magic to steal Tommy's voice! (*Getting her dander up*) Oooh! I'm gonna forget I'm a lady, and belt you one! (*Fuming, she makes for Discord*)

Tommy holds her back

Tommy He's not worth it. (*To Discord*) It isn't very sportsman-like—using magic to win a contest.
Discord Pah! Who cares about that! There's nothing in the rules! And you can't do a thing about it! (*A gloating laugh*) Ha! Ha! Ha!

Dame Well, that's just where you're wrong, you creepy old crook! We *are* gonna do somethin' about it! So there!
Discord (*sneering*) What, break Mother Curseum's spell? *You* can't do that!
Dame (*with bravado*) No, but I know a man who can!
Discord Who?!
Dame (*stumped*) Who…? Er … 'e's… 'ave you ever heard of Harry Potter?
Discord Yes!
Dame Yes, well, our chap's better than 'im! Oh, yes! 'E's a great magician! A mighty, marvellous, magnificent marvel of a magician! Better than your Mother Curseum! 'E'll soon get Tommy's voice back! Oh, yes! (*She looks off* DL) 'Ere 'e comes now! Prepare to be terrified! (*She gestures grandly towards the* DL *entrance*)

Melody enters from DL. *She is supporting a very doddery old man. He has a long white beard, and wears thick lens spectacles. Under one arm he carries a huge book, decorated with magic symbols and signs. He is Professor Wizo*

Wizo (*to Melody, in a quavering voice*) Thank you, my dear. (*He peers about, short-sightedly*) Where exactly are we?

Dame Ditty, Tommy and Benny react. Discord roars with mocking laughter

Discord Ha! Ha! Ha! So this is your terrifying magician! He looks like he needs magic just to stand up! Ha! Ha! Ha!
Melody (*leading Wizo across to the others*) This is Professor Wizo. Professor, I'd like you to meet Dame Ditty.
Wizo (*shaking Tommy's hand*) Very pleased to meet you, madam. (*He shakes Benny's hand*) And you too, young lady.
Dame (*aside to Melody*) What's this? I send you to find a magician, and you come back with Mr Magoo's grandad!
Wizo (*shaking Dame by the hand*) Good day to you, sir.

Laughing his mocking laugh, Discord exits DR

I understand you are in need of my very special services.
Dame (*dubiously*) Are you really a magician?
Wizo Oh, indeed, yes. For many, many, many—many, many years. Professor Wizo at your service! (*He recites his little jingle*) "If you need some necromancy—Wizo is the man to fancy!"
Dame Very catchy! Now, we want you to remove a magic spell cast by a witch called Mother Curseum.
Wizo Mother Curseum? Ah, yes, I have heard of her. A very formidable lady.

Act II, Scene 1

A trifle theatrical, but none the less highly skilled in the black arts. What manner of spell is it?
Tommy She removed my singing voice and transferred it to Benny here.
Wizo I see. A number fifty-two! Mm! A tricky one, but certainly not beyond my capabilities.
Dame (*impatiently*) Well, get on with it then! He needs 'is voice back to sing in a contest this afternoon!
Wizo Oh, I see—yes—certainly! Now—where is my book of spells? (*He looks about*) Oh, dear me! I seem to have mislaid it…
Melody It's under your arm.

During the following, Dame Ditty becomes even more agitated and impatient

Wizo Is it? (*He looks under the other arm*) No, it isn't!

Melody slides the book out and hands it to him

Ah! There it is! You had it all the time. Thank you, young man. (*He opens the book and peers at it very closely*) Now, let me see—oh, dear! This is no good at all! I seem to have brought the Chinese translation!

Tommy turns the book up the right way for him

Ah! That's better! Yes! (*He turns some pages*) Here we are! Now, would the two persons involved stand very close together, face to face.

Tommy and Benny comply

(*Peering*) Are they close together?
Dame If they were any closer it'd be indecent! Get on with it!
Wizo (*raising one hand and speaking in a strong, authoritative voice*)
  O, elements of magic, I summon thee!
  Assist me now in this sorcery!
  Do the things you do so well,
  And help remove the witch's spell!

He reads from the book, while making magic passes at Tommy and Benny

  Hocus pocus and dippydarum!
  Mumbo jumbo and harum scarum!
  The evil spell be gone without trace!
  Return the voice to its rightful place!

He makes a final, elaborate magic pass

Abracadabra!! (*He shuts the book*)
All done!
Dame (*surprised*) What, no flashes, bangs or puffs of smoke?
Wizo Oh, quite unnecessary, I can assure you.
Dame (*excitedly*) Well, go on, Tommy! Don't keep us in suspenders—sing!

Tommy clears his throat and sings. The same atrocious noise comes out! Horrified reaction from all. Benny sings. The glorious sound issues forth

(*Rounding on Wizo*) Nothin's 'appened! They're just the same!
Wizo (*very perplexed*) I... I don't understand! It's always worked before! I really don't know why... (*He looks at his book*) Aha! I see what's happened! This is the *wrong* book! Yes! You see, this is volume *two*, and I should have used volume *three*! Oh, dear me! I am a silly old sorcerer!
Dame You can say that again! Well, don't stand there ditherin' an' dodderin'! Run 'ome and fetch it! Hurry! (*To the audience*) Hurry—ha!
Wizo Yes—yes—at once! (*He dodders away towards Dame Ditty's house*)

Melody heads him off, and guides him towards the DL *exit*

I shall fly like the wind!

Wizo dodders out DL

Dame (*calling after him*) And try to make it back *this* century! (*To the audience*) I think Schumacher's job is safe, don't you! (*To the others*) Oh, 'e's a waste of space!
Tommy I don't think he is. He just brought the wrong book, that's all.
Benny Anyone can make a mistake.
Dame (*rounding on him*) Like your mum and dad, y'mean!

Benny reacts, hangs his head, and slouches out DR

Melody (*calling after him*) Benny...! (*To Dame*) There was no need to take it out on him.
Dame I know! I'm sorry! Blame it on management stress! It'll soon be time for the contest! Suppose Speedy Gonzales doesn't get back in time!

Music plays under, and excited voices and laughter of the Chorus are heard off R

What's that?
Tommy (*looking off* R) It's the Duke and Sophie, with a crowd of people.

Act II, Scene 2 49

Melody They must be on their way to the contest.
Dame (*panicking*) Oooh! Where *is* that old fool?! Where is he?!

All three look anxiously towards the DL *exit, as the Lights fade to Black-out. The music increases in volume and continues during the scene change. The Lights come up on——*

Scene 2

The street

Tabs, or the front cloth used in Act I, Scene 2

Music

The Duke and Sophie enter from DR. *Both are magnificently attired. The Chorus and Children follow them on from* DR *and* DL. *They go straight into a jolly "Come to the Fair" type song, led by Sophie*

Song 14

After the song, the Duke and Sophie exit DL, *followed by the Chorus and Children*

Discord enters from DR, *followed by Mother Curseum. They snarl and sneer at the audience, and are met with the usual barrage of abuse*

Curseum (*to Discord*) They are a cheeky bunch, aren't they! (*She points out someone*) Especially *that* one! I've a good mind to change him into a human being [or something topical]! Hee! Hee! Hee!
Discord Never mind those cretins! I've got a problem.
Curseum Several by the look of it. Y'know I've got a spell to cure ugliness.
Discord Then why haven't you used it on yourself?
Curseum Touché.
Discord Listen. I've got you here because Dame Ditty has called in a magician to remove your spell from Tommy Tucker.
Curseum (*indignantly*) Has she indeed! And who is this magician?
Discord Some doddering old fool called Professor Wizo.
Curseum Wizo! I've heard of him!
Discord He seems completely incompetent, but I didn't want to take any chances. That's why I called you here.
Curseum You did right. A doddering old fool he may be, but he certainly

knows his onions! He's been in the magic trade even longer than I have. And did he break my spell?
Discord I don't know. I came straight to fetch you. I left that idiot Benny there... (*He looks off* DL) Ah! There he is!

Benny enters DL

He sees them and is about to run off, but Discord grabs him

Oh, no, you don't! (*He pushes Benny* C)

Benny cowers between the two nasties

Now! Tell us what happened at Ditty's! Did that old fool Wizo remove the spell on Tommy Tucker?
Benny (*trying to be brave*) I'm not sayin'!

Discord and Curseum each grab one of his ears, twisting them

Discord
Curseum } (*together*) Tell us! Tell us!
Benny (*squirming in agony*) Ahhhgh!! Ooow! Never! Never!
Curseum (*with ghoulish glee*) Leave him alone with me! I've got ways of makin' him talk! I'll change him into a parrot!
Benny Do what you like! My slips are lealed!
Discord Tell us what we want to know, or I'll send Mother Curseum to visit your mother!
Curseum Yes! And I'll take some of my slimy, scaly friends with me! Hee! Hee! Hee!
Benny (*giving in*) All right! All right! I'll tell you!

They release him

'E tried to remove the spell, but it didn't work...

Discord and Curseum laugh

...Because 'e'd brought the wrong spell book. 'E's gone 'ome to fetch the right one. Tha's all I know.
Discord (*pushing Benny to the* DR *exit*) Get back to my house! Don't leave it until I fetch you for the contest! Get out!

Benny pokes his tongue out at them, then exits DR

Act II, Scene 2   51

What are you going to do?

Curseum Simple. I'll steal the book. Without it, old Wizo's about as much use as a glass hammer. His sort always relies on books for castin' spells. Not me! I keep mine in me noddle!

Discord (*looking off* DL) Look! Here he comes now! And he's got the book with him. Shall we jump him and grab it?

Curseum Too risky! He might change himself into Arnie Schwarzanegger! I'll just ask him to give it to me.

Discord But…

Curseum Not as meself—as someone else.

Discord You mean…?

Curseum Yes! (*She moves away to* DR) It's time to become scintillating Sophie again! (*She raises her arms and casts the spell*)
> O, powers of darkness hark to me,
> And aid my work in sorcery!
> Change my form, so coarse and plain,
> And turn me into Miss Sophie again!

There is a flash, followed by a complete Black-out. Mysterious music plays. When the Lights come up, Sophie stands in place of Curseum

Sophie Hee! Hee! Hee! Here we are again! And look—a different dress! (*To Discord*) You hide, an' I'll deal wiv him. Once I've got the book, you grab him an' lock him up somewhere!

They exchange gloating laughs

Discord exits DL

The fake Sophie gets into character

Professor Wizo dodders on from DL. *Under his arm he carries another huge book. He pauses to catch his breath*

Wizo Phew! Oh, dear me! All this rushing about. I hope I'll get there in time. On we go! (*He dodders across*)

Sophie moves down, and pretends to bump into him

Discord partly emerges from hiding, and stands watching

Oh! I do beg your pardon, sir.

Sophie (*in the demure and charming mode*) Please don't apologise. It was my fault entirely.

Wizo (*peering at her*) Oh, it's a young woman. (*He peers even closer*) And a very pretty one too.

Sophie (*aside, to the audience*) Hee! Hee! Hee! (*To him*) You seem to be in a great hurry.

Wizo Yes, my dear, I am. Some people are in urgent need of my services. Goodbye. Nice to meet you. (*He starts to dodder on his way*)

Sophie Can I be of any assistance? That book looks awfully heavy. Would you like me to carry it for you?

Wizo No, thank you, my dear. It's very precious. I mustn't let it out of my sight.

Sophie But it would only be for a few minutes. Just until you reach your destination. Please let me take it. (*She reaches for the book*)

Wizo moves away slightly. Sophie shows her annoyance to the audience

(*Going to him, and taking his arm, very affectionately*) Oh, please let me help you. Let me relieve you of your load.

Wizo (*greatly affected*) I... I... (*Aside, to the audience*) I haven't had an offer like that since I was seventy-five!

Sophie (*slowly reaching for the book*) Let me carry it—I promise I'll take great care of it.

She is just about to grab the book, but Wizo moves away again. Again Sophie shows her annoyance

Wizo I'm not sure... (*To the audience*) What do you think? Should I let her take it?

"No!" from the audience

Sophie (*to the audience, in Curseum mode*) Oh, yes, he should!

"Oh no, he shouldn't!"/"Oh, yes, he should!" routine with the audience follows. Unseen by Wizo, Discord joins in. Finally, Wizo calls a halt

Wizo (*to the audience*) Quiet, please! Quiet! Thank you. (*To Sophie*) I'm sorry, my dear, but the good people think I shouldn't. I'm very sorry.

Sophie pretends to be very upset, and dissolves into a flood of tears

Sophie (*sobbing pitifully*) I ... I was only ... trying to be ... helpful ... boo hoo!

Wizo (*going to her, very concerned*) Oh, dear, dear! (*To the audience*) Now

Act II, Scene 3   53

you've made her cry! (*To Sophie*) There, there, my dear. Please don't upset yourself. Of course you can carry my book. Here you are. (*He holds the book out to her*)

Sophie snatches the book, and holds it up with a hideous peal of triumphant laughter. Thunder and lightning! Dramatic chords of music!

Sophie Hee! Hee! Hee!
Wizo (*shocked and confused*) What is the meaning of this?! Who are you?
Sophie A fellow spellbinder of yours—Mother Curseum, the queen of witches!
Wizo But I thought you were a hideous old hag!
Sophie That's magic for you, mate! Hee! Hee! Hee!
Wizo Give me back my book!
Sophie Not on yer life! Without this book your powers are useless! You and your new-found friends are finished! Tommy Tucker won't be singin' at the contest—*or anywhere else*! Hee! Hee! Hee!

Laughing and sneering at the audience, Sophie exits DR

Wizo (*tottering after her*) Bring it back!
Discord (*grabbing Wizo*) You're not going anywhere, you old fool! You're coming with me! Ha! Ha! Ha!

Laughing and sneering at the audience, Discord drags Wizo out DL, *as the Lights fade to Black-out*

Music to cover the scene change. The sound of a fairground organ (taped) merges with the music, then the Lights come up on——

SCENE 3

The fairground

Bright fairground stalls and booths on each side. Small, colourful flags are hung about. The backcloth shows the rest of the fairground with helter-skelter, ferris wheel and tents, etc., etc. UC *is a platform with three chairs set across the back of it. A large poster reads "GRAND SINGING CONTEST. £1000 PRIZE!" Entrances above and below the side stalls*

The colourful scene is alive with noise and movement. A fairground organ is heard playing (taped)

The Chorus and Children are discovered as spectators, vendors and gaily clad fairfolk. The spectators carry balloons and candyfloss. The vendors peddle their wares, and the fairfolk give displays of their various skills. A fire eater might be nice! To suitable music, a troupe of shapely, bespangled dancers run on and perform as jugglers or tumblers, etc. Singing can accompany the dance display

Song 15

After the number, the Dancers run out

The Crowd disperse upstage to look at stalls, etc. Unobtrusively, the fairground organ plays. It gradually fades out as the scene progresses

The fake Sophie, still clutching the book, creeps on from DR. *She looks furtively about, cackles to the audience, then makes for the exit,* DL

The Duke enters there

Duke Ah, Sophie, m'dear! I was wonderin' where you'd got to... (*He indicates the book*) Egad! What the deuce have you got there?
Sophie Er ... raffle tickets!

Sophie runs past him and out DL

Puzzled, the Duke watches her go, then moves up stage to mingle with the crowd

A couple of shapely Dancers enter from DR. *They move* C, *and stop to adjust their tights*

The Duke spots them, and comes down with a twinkle in his eye. He bows to the Dancers. Giggling, they trot away to the exit DL, *and turn. The Duke waves to them*

Sophie (the real one) enters from DR

Papa...

Giggling, the Dancers exit DL

Duke (*flustered*) I never touched 'em ... what? Oh, Sophie! (*He goes to her*) By Jove! Sold 'em all already?! Well done! Splendid! Splendid! Good show!

Act II, Scene 3   55

The Duke exits DR

Puzzled, Sophie watches him go

Dame Ditty and Tommy enter from DL

They see Sophie and are about to turn tail, when she turns and sees them

Sophie Tommy… Dame Ditty…

Tommy and the Dame turn with sickly grins

Tommy } (*together*) Hallo!
Dame }

During the following, the Chorus, etc., drift out, UR *and* UL

Sophie (*crossing to Tommy and Dame*) It'll soon be time for the contest. Are you feeling nervous?
Dame (*aside to the audience*) She doesn't know the 'alf!
Tommy (*acting nonchalant*) Oh, just a few butterflies in the belly.
Dame (*aside to the audience*) More like a herd of elephants!
Sophie You needn't worry. I'm sure you're going to win with that wonderful voice of yours.

Dame Ditty and Tommy just nod and give sickly grins

Well—I will see you both at the contest. Goodbye and good luck.

Sophie exits DR

Dame (*as soon as Sophie is out of sight*) Luck! We need more than luck! We need International Rescue! Oh, where is that old fool Wizo? 'E should 'ave been back ages ago!
Tommy (*looking off* L) Here's Melody! Perhaps she's found him.

Melody runs on from DL, *out of breath*

Dame (*rushing to her*) Where is 'e?! Where is 'e?!
Melody (*getting her breath back*) I… I don't know! I've looked everywhere! He's completely vanished!
Dame 'E's probably eloped with Puff, the magic dragon! (*Despairingly*) Well, that's it! Bang goes our chance of winnin' that contest. Old Discord'll kop the lot! I might as well emigrate to [local place]!

Tommy I'm sure something has happened to the Professor. I don't think he'd let us down.
Dame (*fuming*) Well, 'e 'as, 'asn't 'e! Professor Wizo! I'll Wiz 'im! If I ever see that dodderin' old duffer again, I'll ... I'll...

A dusty, cobweb-covered Wizo enters from DR, *supported by Benny*

(*Seeing Wizo and changing her mood completely*) ...welcome 'im with open arms! Professor! (*She rushes across as if to hug Wizo, then reacts to his condition*) Ugh! Yuck! What 'ave you been doin'?
Benny Dr Discord 'ad 'im locked up in the cellar! I've just let 'im out. I'd better get back before my abscess is discovered!

Benny runs out DR

Tommy and Melody bring Wizo C. *They dust him off and remove the cobwebs*

Dame This is no time for spring cleanin'! (*To Wizo*) Work the spell! Get Tommy 'is voice back!
Wizo I'm afraid I can't.
Others What!
Wizo Not without my book of spells. It's impossible.
Melody But we thought you went home to get it, Professor.
Wizo I did, my dear. But it was stolen from me on the way here.
Dame By that dirty old Discord?
Wizo I'm sure it was at his instigation. But, the actual thief was Mother Curseum herself. Well, when I say herself, it wasn't. She'd transformed herself into a beautiful young woman.
Tommy Sophie again!
Wizo I must admit I fell for her charms and ... and actually gave the book to her. It was very stupid of me. (*He sighs*) There's no fool like an old fool.
Dame (*to the audience*) And they don't come any older, folks!

Unseen by them, the fake Sophie creeps on from DR, *still clutching the book. She sees the group, and quickly gets into character as Sophie. She walks demurely across, in front of them*

Sophie (*as she passes them*) Good afternoon.
Others (*politely*) Good afternoon.

Sophie exits DL

Wizo (*reacting*) That voice! It's her! The one who stole my book! After her! Don't let her get away!

Act II, Scene 3   57

To suitable "hurry" music, a chase sequence follows. It gradually builds in momentum, until by the end, everyone is chasing around at a break neck speed. (Strobe lighting may be used if desired)

Wizo dodders out DL. *The others follow him out. Sophie runs on from* UL, *and out* DR. *The others chase after her, and out* DR. *Sophie runs on from* UR, *and out* DL. *The others follow her on and off. Wizo and the others run on from* DL, *now being chased by Sophie. They realize their mistake, turn and chase Sophie out* DL. *The Duke and a couple of the Chorus enter from* UR. *Sophie runs on from* DL, *hotly pursued by Wizo and the others. They all run out* DR. *The Duke, seeing what he thinks is his daughter in trouble, gives chase himself, followed by the Chorus members. Sophie runs on from* UR, *pursued by all the others. The sniffing Boy and a few more of the Chorus have joined the chase. The chase continues until the entire Chorus have joined in, and the stage is just a blur of running figures. Finally, it ends with Dame Ditty, Tommy, Melody and Wizo staggering on alone. All are exhausted and out of breath*

(Take out strobe lighting if used) The "hurry" music continues. Comic business as Dame Ditty, unable to speak, signals "cut" to the pianist/band. The music stops

Tommy (*getting his breath back*) I think she's given us the slip!
Dame (*contortions with her costume*) I think I've lost mine!

The real Sophie enters from DR. *She is supporting the Duke, who is exhausted and mopping his brow*

Sophie (*concerned*) Are you all right, Papa? What on earth have you been doing?
Duke (*gasping*) Need you ask! (*To the others*) What the devil d'you mean by chasin' me daughter around the fairground?
Sophie (*obviously puzzled*) Chasing me? What do you mean?
Wizo (*reacting*) That voice again! It's her! (*He stumps over and confronts Sophie, angrily*) Give me back that book, you treacherous hag!

Sophie is obviously shocked and bewildered. The Duke is outraged

Duke Zounds, sirrah! How dare you speak to my daughter like that!
Wizo She's a witch!
Duke (*exploding*) What!!

Tommy hastily pulls Wizo away

Tommy (*whispering to Wizo*) That's not her. *She's* the *real* one! (*He passes Wizo on to the Dame and Melody, then turns back to the Duke*) I'm sorry about that, your Grace. It's the rain. It always affects him.
Duke Rain? But we ain't had any rain!
Tommy Exactly—it's the lack of it! (*Hastily*) Have you both seen the merry-go-round? It's truly remarkable. No? Then allow me to show it to you. This way.

Before they can object, Tommy hustles the Duke and Sophie out DR. *As he goes he gives the others a "do something" look*

Dame (*rounding on Wizo*) This is all *your* fault!
Wizo I'm most terribly sorry.
Melody Isn't there *anything* you can do, Professor?
Wizo Alas no, my dear. Without my book of spells I am completely and utterly helpless.
Dame (*to the audience*) Trust us to pick a wonky wizard!
Melody We can't give up. There's still time. We *must* get your book back. (*To the audience*) You'll help us find it, won't you?

"Yes!" from the audience

Dame (*to the audience*) If you see it, you'll give us a shout, won't ya?

"Yes!" from the audience

Unseen by the others, the fake Sophie creeps on from UR. *She is still clutching the book*

The audience start shouting

(*To the audience*) What's up? Is it the book?

"Yes!" from the audience

Melody (*to the audience*) Can you see it?

"Yes!" from the audience. The players look everywhere except behind them

Dame (*to the audience*) Well, I can't see it! Where is it?

"Behind you!" from the audience

Behind us? (*To the others*) You hear that! It's behind us! Let's look!

Act II, Scene 3   59

Sophie quickly exits UL

The others look upstage, then turn back to the audience

> (*To the audience*) There's nothin' there! You lot are 'avin' us on! Stop messin' about! This is very serious, y'know!

Mother Curseum, now back to abnormal, creeps on from UL. *She still clutches the book*

The audience start shouting again

> (*To the others*) They're at it again! Take no notice! (*To the audience*) You're just playin' tricks! (*Etc.*)

Curseum creeps down and lurks behind them. The audience continue to shout

Melody (*to Dame*) I think they really mean it this time.
Wizo (*to Dame*) Yes, they seem in earnest.
Dame Right! (*To the audience*) We're gonna look! And woe betide you lot if there's nothin' there!

Close together, they circle round with Curseum keeping behind them. This business is repeated a couple of times. Finally, they turn and come face to face with the witch. With a startled yell, they scatter. Dame to R, *Wizo and Melody to* L. *Curseum remains* C. *She holds up the book, and gives her hideous laugh*

Curseum Hee! Hee! Hee!
Wizo My book! Get it!

Curseum makes for the exit DR, *but Dame Ditty heads her off. Curseum makes for the exit* DL, *but Melody and Wizo get there before her and bar the way*

Curseum (*backing away to* C, *with a snarl*) You fools! Do you think you can pit your puny wits against mine!
Dame Never mind our puny bits! 'And over that book!

The three advance on Curseum. She backs away and clutches the book even tighter

Curseum Never! It's mine now! I've been tryin' to get a copy of it for ages! WH Smith [or local newsagents] are hopeless! With this book I shall further my career in diabolical dastardliness!

Wizo You mean—you intend to use it for your own purposes?
Curseum (*hugging the book*) I do!

Wizo starts chuckling. It develops into a peal of almost insane laughter. The others react

Dame (*to the audience*) 'E's flipped!
Wizo (*regaining control of himself*) Oh, dear! Oh, dear! I haven't heard anything so funny since Merlin sat on Excalibur by mistake! (*To Curseum*) *You* using that book! The idea! (*He starts chuckling again*)
Curseum (*snarling at him*) What d'you mean, you old fool? Are you sayin' I can't read!
Wizo Not from that book, you can't. I imagine you're still on chapter one of "Magic Made Easy". To be able to read spells from that particular book, you need special skills which *you* don't possess, Mother Curseum.
Curseum Ha! We'll soon see about that! (*She opens the book at random*) I'll show ya! (*She reads from the book*)
  By the power of wizards, elves and witches!
  May you be plagued by a thousand itches!

She makes a magic pass at Dame Ditty. Comic business as Dame Ditty yells, and starts scratching uncontrollably. Curseum gives a laugh of triumph. After a while, the itching subsides and Dame Ditty stands there, panting

Curseum (*to Wizo, smugly*) There!
Wizo Oh, that was an easy one. Try ... er ... page two hundred and one ... er ... spell number thirteen. I bet you can't cast that one.
Curseum (*very cockily*) Just you wait! (*She finds the page in the book*) 'Ere we go! (*She reads*)
  Hocus pocus and ice cold beer!
  Make me vanish and disappear!

There is a blinding flash and a puff of smoke. A complete Black-out follows. Mysterious music plays under. There is a cry from Curseum, which gradually fades away into silence. When the Lights come up, the witch has vanished from the scene. The book lies on the ground in the place where she stood

Dame Crikey! She's gorn an' gorn!
Wizo (*pleased with himself*) Yes, and forever, I'm glad to say.
Melody But what did you do, Professor?
Wizo Oh, it was quite simple, my dear. I tricked her into reading a spell for self-destruction.
Melody How clever! Well done! Well done!

Act II, Scene 3

Dame Never mind 'andin' out the Oscars! (*She picks up the book and thrusts it at Wizo*) 'Ere's yer book! Now get Tommy 'is voice back!
Wizo (*finding the place in the book*) Of course ... of course ... now, would the two persons involved stand very close together, face to face.
Dame They'll 'ave a job! They're not 'ere! (*To Melody*) Quick, run and find Tommy and Benny...

Suddenly, a bell is heard ringing off L. *The sniffing Boy enters from* DL, *ringing a large hand bell. He is followed by the Duke and Sophie. With them is a distinguished-looking individual, either male or female. (It might be nice to persuade a well-known local personality to play this part!) At the same time, all the Chorus enter and fill the sides*

The Boy continues to ring his bell

Duke (*to the ensemble, above the noise of the bell*) My friends! It is now time... (*To the Boy*) You can stop that now!

The Boy stops ringing the bell and gives a loud sniff

(*To the ensemble*) My friends! It is now time for the grand singing contest to begin!

Loud cheers from the crowd, as the Duke, Sophie and the distinguished guest go up stage and mount the platform. They arrange themselves on the three chairs. The Boy stands near the platform, with his bell poised. Subdued chatter from the crowd. Dame Ditty, Melody and Wizo huddle together downstage, and speak in hushed tones

Dame It's too late! We're done for!
Melody There must be something you can do, Professor.
Wizo There's just one chance. I'll read the spell and hope that it works at long distance. I can't guarantee anything...
Dame (*desperately*) Just do it!
Wizo (*reading in hushed tones*)
        Mumbo jumbo and harum-scarum!
        Hocus pocus and dippydarum!
        The evil spell be gone without trace!
        Return the voice to its rightful place!
        Abracadabra!
(*To the others*) Fingers crossed!

With fingers crossed on both hands, the three clear to DL

The Duke rises and taps the Boy on the shoulder. He rings his bell loudly. The Crowd go silent and turn their attention to the platform

Discord enters from DR, *dragging Benny with him*

The Duke taps the Boy on the shoulder and he stops ringing the bell. Silence

Duke (*to the ensemble*) Ladies and gentlemen...

Loud sniff from the Boy

Er... *and* children. The exciting moment you have all been waiting for has finally arrived! The grand singing contest between the music schools of Dr Discord... (*He gestures to Discord*)

Discord gives an elaborate bow. Suppressed groans and boos from the Crowd

...and Dame Ditty! (*He gestures to Dame*)

Dame Ditty gives an awkward curtsy. Cheers and applause from the Crowd

First, may I introduce our illustrious guest and judge of the contest—Doctor Dulcet Tone of the [local] Music Academy [or some other local reference]! (*He starts the applause*)

The judge rises, takes a bow and sits back down

And now, without further ado—are the contestants ready?
Discord (*dragging Benny forward*) Mine is!
Duke And yours, Dame Ditty?
Dame (*flustered*) Well... I... I...
Discord (*sneering*) He's afraid to show his face!
Dame Oh, no, 'e isn't!
Discord Oh, yes, he is!

"Oh, no, he isn't!"/"Oh, yes, he is!" routine with the audience follows. The Chorus join in, taking Dame Ditty's side. Finally, the Duke seizes the bell, and rings it himself. All go silent

Duke Dame Ditty, where is your contestant? Where is Tommy Tucker?
Dame (*aside*) That's what I'd like to know!
Melody I'm sure he'll be here at any moment, your Grace.

Act II, Scene 3 63

Duke I see—well—in that case, we shall begin with Dr Discord's contestant. (*To Benny*) Be so good as to mount the platform.
Benny (*to Discord*) I didn't know I 'ad to catch a train!

Discord pushes Benny on to the platform, then returns to DR. *Benny is very nervous and bashful*

Duke (*to Benny*) Will you give us your name?
Benny No.
Duke Why not?
Benny 'Cos I need it meself!

Laughter from the Crowd

Duke (*trying to be patient*) What are you called?
Benny Lots of fings... (*He glances towards Discord*) Some of 'em not very nice. My maiden name's Benny!
Duke I see. And what are you going to sing for us, Benny?
Benny [The chosen song]!
Duke Very well! Off you go!

Benny starts to leave the platform

The Duke stops him

No! No! I mean, off you go—with your song! (*He sits back down*)

The intro. Music plays as Benny adopts an "operatic" stance. Spotlight on him. Dame Ditty and the others are on tenter hooks, with all fingers crossed. Benny takes a deep breath, and sings. His voice is back to its former off-key awfulness

Song 15a (Short Reprise of Song 3)

This only needs to be a short reprise. Just enough to establish that the spell has been broken. Benny is shocked, but struggles on bravely. The Crowd groan and cover their ears. Discord is beside himself with disbelief and rage. Naturally, Dame Ditty and the others are overjoyed. She shakes Wizo's hand and slaps him on the back. Benny finishes singing and takes a bow. The spotlight fades out. Little, if any, applause from the the Crowd. The Duke rises to move to Benny

Dame (*to the others*) It worked! It worked!

Melody Yes—but where's Tommy?
Duke (*to Benny; at a loss for words*) Yes—well—er—thank you. You may leave the platform.

Nervously, Benny returns to Discord. During the following, Discord rounds on him, demanding some explanation. Benny can only shrug helplessly

Dame Ditty, has *your* contestant arrived yet?
Dame (*flustered*) I ... he...
Discord Your Grace, it must be obvious that Tommy Tucker has no intention of taking part. As *my* contestant had the good grace to attend, I think it only right that I ... er ... *he* should be declared the winner!

Cries of dissension from the Crowd

Duke (*silencing the Crowd*) One moment—*please*! (*He confers with the judge, then turns back to the ensemble*) Under the circumstances, the judge agrees with Dr Discord.

More outcry from the Crowd. Discord rubs his hands, and laughs gloatingly

Dame But...
Duke I'm sorry, Dame Ditty. But as you've failed to produce a contestant, I have no alternative. (*To the ensemble*) I therefore declare the winner of this contest to be——
Sophie (*jumping up and pointing off* L) Wait, Papa! Look! It's Tommy!

All look, as Tommy enters through the Crowd, L

Discord (*snarling*) He's too late! He's too late!
Duke (*flustered*) I ... I...
Sophie Papa, you hadn't actually announced the winner, had you? Let Tommy sing!

Cries of agreement from the Crowd

Discord (*yelling*) I protest!!
Duke Tommy Tucker, do you still wish to enter this singing contest?
Dame Yes, 'e does! (*Aside to Tommy giving him the thumbs up sign*) You're all right again!
Tommy Yes, your Grace, I certainly do!
Duke Then mount the platform and sing for us!

The Duke and Sophie sit down. Tommy goes on to the platform

Act II, Scene 3   65

Discord I protest!!
All (*to Discord*) Oh, be quiet!!

The intro. Music plays. Spotlight on Tommy. He takes a breath, and sings. His voice has returned to its former magnificence

Song 16

A not too sugary love song. At first, Tommy sings to the ensemble, then he brings Sophie to join him and sings the remainder of the song to her. When it ends, he takes a bow. Tumultuous applause and cheering from everyone—everyone except for Discord, of course! The spotlight fades out. The Duke quickly confers with the Judge, then holds up his hands for silence

Duke Ladies and gentlemen! Our judge has come to a decision, and it gives me great pleasure to announce the winner of this singing contest! And the winner is—Tommy Tucker of Dame Ditty's School!

More applause and cheering. The Duke presents Tommy with a large red money bag, and shakes his hand. They all leave the platform and move forward. Dame Ditty and the others rush to congratulate Tommy. He gives her the money bag. She holds it up with one hand and Tommy's arm with the other. Renewed cheering and applause. Benny applauds wildly. Fuming, Discord grabs him by his ear, and twists it

Benny (*yelling in agony*) Ahooow!!
Discord You!! This is all your fault!

Tommy rushes across, grabs Discord by his ear and twists it. Yelling, he releases Benny, who runs to Melody. Tommy forces Discord to the ground

Tommy (*standing over him*) There! That'll teach you to use black magic on me!
Duke Black magic? Egad, what is all this about?
Dame That rotten rascal got Mother Curseum, the witch, to 'elp 'im win the contest!
Melody He got her to cast a spell which removed Tommy's singing voice and transformed it to Benny.
Dame An' if it 'adn't bin for our friend Professor Wizo 'ere, it would 'ave worked!

Outcry from the Crowd

Discord (*getting to his feet, and snarling at them*) It's not true!

Others Oh, yes, it is! (*To the audience*) Isn't it?

"Yes" from the audience

Discord (*to the audience*) Oh, no, it isn't!

"Oh, yes, it is!"/"Oh, no, it isn't!" routine follows between Discord and the Cast and the audience. Finally, the Duke gets the Boy to ring his bell for silence

Duke I find this incredible—unbelievable!
Benny It's all true, your lordfulship. I work for 'im, and I'm too thick to tell lies!
Duke That I do believe! (*Turning on Discord*) You, sir, are a blackguard and a scoundrel! Leave this town at once, and never show your face here again!

Cries of approval from the others and the Crowd

Discord (*sneering*) And *if* I refuse?
Duke I will have you imprisoned—*or*—I will turn you over to *them*! (*He indicates the audience. To the audience*) I'm sure *you'd* love to deal with him, wouldn't you?

Response from the audience, encouraged by Dame Ditty and the others. Discord snarls back a few times, then gives in

Discord Very well! I'll leave! At least I'll get even with *you*! (*He points to Benny*) If I go, so does your cottage! You and your wretched mother will be homeless! (*Evil, gloating laughter*) Ha! Ha! Ha! Ha!

Benny is very upset by this, and is comforted by Melody

Sophie Papa, we have an empty cottage on the estate. Couldn't Benny and his mother live there?
Duke A capital idea, Sophie! Of course! And I'll give him a job as well!

Foiled, Discord stamps his foot in anger

Benny (*to Duke*) Thank you, your nobleness!
Duke A job where you can sing to your heart's content!
All (*incredlously*) Eh?!!
Duke In my cornfields! I'll save a fortune on scarecrows! (*He turns to Discord*) Are you still here! Go!!

Act II, Scene 4 67

Amid boos and hisses, Discord exits DR—*but not without a final snarl at everyone, including the audience*

All's well that ends well, eh! Come, Tommy! Why don't you lead us all in a celebratory song and dance!
All (*cheering*) Hooray!!

Song 17

Led by Tommy and Sophie, everyone goes into a lively song and dance. Benny and Melody dance together. Dame Ditty grabs the Duke for a partner, and Wizo claims one of the shapely young Dancers. The number ends with a tableau

Tabs, or a front cloth is lowered

Scene 4

The singing lesson

Tabs, or the front cloth used in Act II, Scene 2

Benny's atrocious singing is heard off stage. He enters from DR, *in full blast. He moves in* C, *and ends on an awful, cracked top note*

Benny (*waving to the audience*) Oh, hallo, folks! Hi kids! My singin's getting better, don't you think? (*Ad lib to the audience responses*) I know I'm not as good as Tommy yet, I've got to keep practisin'. (*He starts singing again*)

Melody rushes on from DR, *and Dame Ditty from* DL

Dame (*shouting above his din*) Oy! Oy! Oy! Stop that row!

Benny stops

We've been gettin' complaints from [local reference]!
Benny But I need to practise! (*He starts singing again*)

Dame Ditty clamps her hand over his mouth. Comic business as she keeps taking it away, faster and faster, until his singing sounds like a Red Indian war cry. With disgust, she wipes her hand on his front

Melody He wants to be able to sing like Tommy.
Benny Yeah! (*To Dame*) Will you 'elp me out?
Dame Certainly! Y'see that door marked exit?
Benny (*eagerly*) Yeah!
Dame Go straight through it!
Benny I mean, will you give me a singin' lesson?
Dame Ha! That'd be like gettin' William Hague to grow hair [or other topical/local gag]! (*To the audience*) D'you think I should?

"Yes!" from the audience

Do you really?

"Yes!" from the audience

You'll wish you 'adn't said that! 'Cos I'm gonna get you lot singin' as well! Ha! Ha! It's too late now! (*To Benny*) Right then, Pavagrotti! 'Ave you got the sheets?
Benny Not this week!
Dame I mean the *song sheets*, you wally!
Melody (*looking off*) Here it comes now!

The song sheet is lowered, or can be brought on by the sniffing Boy and Primrose

The House Lights come up

Song 18

They have fun getting Benny and the audience to sing. Children can be brought on to the stage if desired. After, the song sheet is removed and the children return to their seats. Take out House Lights

Dame Ditty, Benny and Melody run out, waving goodbye to the audience, as the Lights fade to Black-out

A fanfare, and the Lights come up on——

Scene 5

The Finale

A special Finale setting or the fairground scene can be used

Act II, Scene 5

Bright Lighting and bouncy music

All enter for the walk down and bows

Tommy   My singing voice has been returned.
Sophie   Despite the witch's spell.
Duke   The winning place you justly earned,
              And my daughter's hand as well.
Benny   I'll practise singin' night an' day!
Melody   I'll help with hugs and kisses.
Benny   I'll join a choir right away!
Dame (*to the audience*) We'll need some ear plugs, missus!
Curseum   I'm back, you see, as large as life!
              (*to Discord*) I rather fancy you, sir!
Discord   I wouldn't mind you for a wife,
              If you changed to Michelle Pfeiffer!
Wizo (*to Dancer*) I may be old and rather spent,
              But I haven't lost my magic!
Dame   Let's hope his magic wand ain't bent,
              That really would be tragic!
              You've been a smashin' audience,
              First rate and very pukka.
              There's only one thing left to say——
All (*waving*) Goodbye—from Tommy Tucker!

Finale Song (Reprise)

CURTAIN

FURNITURE AND PROPERTY LIST

Further dressing may be added at the director's discretion

ACT I

Scene 1

On stage: Town backcloth
Town wings
Dame Ditty's house with hanging sign reading "DAME DITTY. SINGING LESSONS GIVEN"
Dr Discord's house with sign reading "DOCTOR DISCORD. R.A.M. SUPERIOR TEACHER OF MUSIC AND SINGING"
Banner reading "FAIR! TODAY!"

Off stage: Bucket and rag (**Benny**)
Sweets (**Melody**)
Bag (**Sophie**)

Personal: **Discord:** two-headed coin
Tommy: hat

Scene 2

On stage: Tabs, or frontcloth
Poster advertising fair, with "PLUS—GRAND SINGING CONTEST" sticker

Scene 3

On stage: Woodland backcloth
Woodland wings and groundrow
Cave entrance. *On it*: bell push
Clump of bushes
Large picnic hamper
Large tablecloth. *On it*: remains of picnic

Furniture and Property List   71

Off stage: Large cauldron on wheels. *In it*: smoke effect, bottle of green liquid;
              large black box. *In it*: empty bottle, various edible items, box of salt,
              long wooden spoon (**Primrose**)

Personal: **Discord:** wallet of notes
              Duke: handkerchief

ACT II

Scene 1

On stage: Countryside backcloth showing fairground in distance
              Garden wings
              Large tree
              Back of **Dame Ditty**'s house
              Low fence with gate in centre

Off stage: Large magic book (**Wizo**)

Scene 2

On stage: Tabs, or frontcloth used in Act I, Scene 2

Off stage: 2nd large magic book (**Wizo**)

Scene 3

On stage: Backcloth showing fairground
              Bright fairground stalls and booths
              Platform. *On it*: 3 chairs
              Large banner or poster reading "GRAND SINGING CONTEST.
                £1000 PRIZE!"
              Small colourful flags, etc.

Off stage: Balloons, candy floss (**Spectators**)
              Trays (**Vendors**)
              Jugging apparatus, etc. (**Fair folk**)
              2nd magic book (**Sophie**)
              Large hand bell (**Boy**)

Personal: **Duke:** handkerchief
              Duke: large red money bag

Scene 4

On stage: Tabs, or frontcloth used in Act II, Scene 2

Off stage: Song sheet (**SM or member of cast**)

Scene 5

On stage: Special Finale setting or Act II, Scene 2 can be used

LIGHTING PLOT

Property fittings required: nil
Various exterior settings

ACT I, SCENE 1

To open: General exterior lighting

Cue 1   **Melody**: "…be nice enough to help us out."   (Page 13)
Bring up house lights

Cue 2   **Dame** and **Melody** return to stage   (Page 14)
Fade out house lights

Cue 3   Song 5   (Page 16)
Romantic lighting with follow spot on **Tommy** *and* **Sophie**,
at end of song take out spot, return to previous lighting

Cue 4   End of Song 6   (Page 19)
Fade lights to black-out

ACT I, SCENE 2

To open: General exterior lighting

Cue 5   **Discord** exits   (Page 25)
Fade lights to black-out

ACT I, SCENE 3

To open: Sunny woodland lighting

Cue 6   2nd peal of laughter from cave   (Page 28)
Dark and sinister lighting

Cue 7	**Benny** presses bell third time *Flash of lightning, weird lights flashing across stage, then return to previous sinister lighting*	(Page 29)
Cue 8	Song 10 *Eerie follow spots on **Dancers**, fade out at end of song*	(Page 29)
Cue 9	**Demons** kneel at cave *Flash of lightning, green spot on cave*	(Page 29)
Cue 10	**Discord** moves to **Curseum** *Fade out green spot on **Curseum***	(Page 29)
Cue 11	**Curseum** raises arms and cackles *Dim sinister lighting and bring up green spot on cauldron area*	(Page 32)
Cue 12	**Curseum** makes magic pass and cackles *Flash of lightning, weird lights flash across stage*	(Page 32)
Cue 13	**Curseum**: "Cut!!" *Instantly cut lightning and flashing lights, return to previous sinister lighting and green spot on cauldron*	(Page 32)
Cue 14	**Curseum**: "Behold—the magic potion!" *Fade out green spot, bring up general sinister lighting*	(Page 32)
Cue 15	**Curseum**: "Right! Here goes then!" *Fade lighting down, green spot on **Curseum***	(Page 33)
Cue 16	**Curseum**: "…into the Duke's fair daughter!" *Flash, followed by black-out. When **Curseum/Sophie** switch complete, return to sunny woodland lighting*	(Page 33)
Cue 17	**Sophie**: "…watchin' "Big Brother"! Hee! Hee! Hee!" *Fade lighting down, bring up spot on **Tommy** and **Benny***	(Page 35)
Cue 18	**Benny** gives a huge swallow *Fade out spot and return to bright woodland lighting*	(Page 36)
Cue 19	**Chorus** and **Pupils** exit *Fade lighting down for dark and sinister effect, bring up "evil" spot on **Discord***	(Page 39)

Lighting Plot

Cue 20	**Discord** and **Benny** exit, **Curseum** enters *Transfers spot to* **Curseum**	(Page 39)
Cue 21	**Curseum**: "Let's give them hell! Hee! Hee! Hee!" *Flashes of lightning. Red, flickering lights fill the stage*	(Page 39)

ACT II, SCENE 1

To open:	General exterior lighting	
Cue 22	**All** look anxiously towards DL exit *Fade lights to black-out*	(Page 49)

ACT II, SCENE 2

To open:	General exterior lighting	
Cue 23	Song 14 *Spot on* **Sophie**, *fade out at end of song*	(Page 49)
Cue 24	**Curseum**: "And turn me into Miss Sophie again!" *Flash, followed by black-out. After* **Curseum/Sophie** *switch return to previous lighting*	(Page 51)
Cue 25	**Sophie** holds up book and laughs *Flash of lightning*	(Page 53)
Cue 26	**Discord** drags **Wizo** out *Fade lights to black-out*	(Page 53)

ACT II, SCENE 3

To open:	Bright general exterior lighting	
Cue 27	Song 15 *Follow spot on* **Dancers**, *fade out at end of song*	(Page 54)
Cue 28	Chase sequence *Strobe lighting (optional)*	(Page 57)

Cue 29	**Dame Ditty**, **Tommy**, **Melody** and **Wizo** stagger on *Take out strobe lighting if used, return to previous lighting*	(Page 57)
Cue 30	**Curseum**: "Make me vanish and disappear!" *Flash, followed by black-out. Allow Curseum to exit, then return to previous lighting*	(Page 60)
Cue 31	Song 15a (Reprise of Song 3) *Spot on **Benny**, at end of song fade out spot*	(Page 63)
Cue 32	Song 16 *Spot on **Tommy**, at end of song fade out spot*	(Page 65)

ACT II, SCENE 4

To open:	Overall general lighting	
Cue 33	Song sheet is lowered or brought on *Bring up house lights, spot on song sheet*	(Page 68)
Cue 34	Children from audience return to seats *Fade out house lights*	(Page 68)
Cue 35	**Dame Ditty**, **Benny** and **Melody** exit *Fade lights to black-out*	(Page 68)

ACT II, SCENE 5 (FINALE)

To open: Bright lighting

No cues

EFFECTS PLOT

ACT I

Cue 1	**Duke**: "It's so peaceful and quiet." *Peal of cackling laughter echoes from cave*	(Page 27)
Cue 2	**Dame** exits *Repeat cackling laughter from cave*	(Page 28)
Cue 3	**Benny** presses bell first time *Eerie organ music echoes from cave*	(Page 29)
Cue 4	**Benny** presses bell second time *Repeat organ music from cave*	(Page 29)
Cue 5	**Benny** presses bell third time *Thunder clap, howling wind and weird sounds, groud mist from cave*	(Page 29)
Cue 6	**Demons** kneel at cave *Thunder clap, ground mist from cave*	(Page 29)
Cue 7	**Primrose** enters with cauldron *Smoke effect in cauldron*	(Page 31)
Cue 8	**Curseum** makes magic pass and cackles *Blinding flash and puff of smoke in or near the cauldron. Rolls of thunder and weird sounds*	(Page 32)
Cue 9	**Curseum**: "Cut!!" *Instantly cut thunder and weird sounds*	(Page 32)
Cue 10	**Curseum**: "…into the Duke's fair daughter!" *Blinding flash and puff of smoke*	(Page 33)
Cue 11	**Tommy** and **Benny** open their mouths wide *Strange, tinkling sounds*	(Page 36)

Cue 12	**Benny** gives a huge swallow *Fade out tinkling sounds*	(Page 36)
Cue 13	**Curseum**: "Let's give them hell!" *Rolls of thunder, howling winds, weird sounds and ground mist*	(Page 39)

ACT II

Cue 14	**Curseum**: "And turn me into Miss Sophie again!" *Blinding flash and puff of smoke*	(Page 51)
Cue 15	**Sophie** holds up book and laughs *Thunder clap*	(Page 53)
Cue 16	During change to Scene 3 *Taped fairground organ, continuing into Scene 3, fade out as scene progresses*	(Page 53)
Cue 17	**Curseum**: "Make me vanish and disappear!" *Blinding flash and puff of smoke*	(Page 60)

MADE AND PRINTED IN GREAT BRITAIN BY
LATIMER TREND & COMPANY LTD PLYMOUTH
MADE IN ENGLAND

www.ingramcontent.com/pod-product-compliance
Ingram Content Group UK Ltd.
Pitfield, Milton Keynes, MK11 3LW, UK
UKHW021844210426
5322IPUK00022B/455